CW00499997

Coincidences: Towards a Greater Understanding

Tony Crisp is the author of twelve books on various aspects of people's mental and spiritual growth. Since 1955 he has explored, taught and written about self-help ways you can disco ver your own wider experience of body and mind. His book *The New Dream Dictionary* has been published in more than eight countries. Tony helped found one of the first centres for exploring human potential in the UK. His thirty years of experience in helping people allow their spontaneous inner life to emerge creatively, and his work with dreams, adds to his depth of expression in writing about coincidences.

Alternatives
Life Options for Today

Other titles in the *Alternatives* series are:

Astrology and Childhood Peter West
Dreams and Dreaming: Understanding Your Sleep Messages Tony Crisp
Educate Your Memory: Memory Improvements for Students of All Ages Billy Roberts
Feng Shui Hour by Hour: Change Your Day J. M. Sertori
The Message of the Hands Peter West
Pen Pictures: Interpreting the Secrets of Handwriting Peter West
Perfume Power Joules Taylor
Personal Progress Through Positive Thinking Hilary Jones and Frank Gilbert
The Power of Peace: The Value of Meditation Shirley Wallis
Tarot for Today Ken Taylor
Visitation: The Certainty of Alien Activity Peter Hough
Working Memory: Improving Your Memory for the Workplace Billy Roberts

Coincidences:

Towards a Greater Understanding

TONY CRISP

LONDON
HOUSE

First published in Great Britain in 2000 by
LONDON HOUSE
114 New Cavendish Street
London W1M 7FD

A catalogue record for this book is available
from the British Library

ISBN 1 902809 17 3

Edited and designed by DAG Publications Ltd, London.
Printed and bound by Biddles Limited,
Guildford, Surrey.

To YOU
With whom I am
Intricately interwoven
Now
Forever

Contents

Preface

When something as strange as a striking coincidence happens to you, or someone near you, it confronts you with the inexplicable. There are usually no visible links between the event and your environment. A powerful coincidence often gives you no rational clues either, unless perhaps you look beyond logical thought. Therefore a radical coincidence is a doorway for one's mind and heart to move beyond limiting attitudes and beliefs. The chapters following will bring the inexplicable closer to you, so you can look at it, hold it, wonder at it. Then you will be led to see that perhaps there are faint pathways in the strangeness of coincidence.

By gaining a glimpse of the architecture of the extraordinary, you might dare to explore its rooms and vistas. Certainly you will be made aware that there is more to your life than you had perhaps imagined. The book will even show you how to leave the door open for that *More* to enter your own experience.

Acknowledgements

I have gained an enormous amount of help from certain authors. Not only have they ploughed this field before me, making the going easier, but their contact with people all over the world has provided a wealth of information and evidence.

In particular, thanks to Ken Anderson for the years of work that are evident in his book *Coincidences*; to Victor Mansfield for the searching thought and enquiry shedding light on the psychological and scientific connections with synchronicity, as expressed in his book *Synchronicity and Soul-Making*; and to Alan Vaughan for the immense number of cases described in his book *Incredible Coincidences*.

Thanks to Melvin Morse, MD, and Paul Perry for their book *Closer to the Light*. Not only has the book given valuable material, but it has been inspiring to me personally.

Eddie Boucher shared some of his collected cases of synchronicity with me, and so added significantly to the book. Several local BBC Radio studios were good enough to give me time talking about coincidences, and thereby enabling me to hear many people's experiences. Special thanks to Jenny Walmsley, Anna Murray and Alan Wright.

Thanks particularly to Rod Dymott and Chelsey Fox, for being instrumental in my writing this book.

1
The Ghost in the Machine

When a striking coincidence occurs to you, it is more than a chance event. It is a breakthrough of something that science is only on the edge of understanding. It is an emergence into your life of a power that transcends the common concept of time and space. It is the working of something that can transform your love, your work, your creativity, and your way of viewing life.

Whether we call it coincidence, chance or synchronicity, things happen to us that are inexplicable. How, for instance, did you meet your partner, or the people who are important in your life? Why is it that when you are exploring an idea or searching for help, a book almost leaps off the shelf of a shop or library? Then, when examining the book, you find it is the very friend or instructor you need. Where did your most creative acts emerge from? Almost certainly they were surrounded by synchronistic events. All these aspects of your life have introduced you to coincidences, but perhaps you haven't looked deep into the face of this wonderful colleague.

A coincidence is not simply meeting an old friend in a very unusual setting, or discovering you have the same birth date and name as someone you accidentally meet at a party. A coincidence can be something we feel within us, that then links with an outward event. Therefore synchronicity can also arise through a dream, an intuition or a near-death experience. The mystery of such experiences touches us in every department of our life.

At the end of World War Two, when I was nine years of age, my parents moved from the countryside back to London. My paternal grandfather owned a greengrocery shop in a small street called Woburn Walk. This was in a quiet side turning behind St Pancras Church. My grandfather had moved from Italy to London with his wife Rafaela in the early part of the century. At the end of the war he wanted to return to Italy to visit relatives. Rafaela had died several years previously, so he went alone. His parting seemed easy. My father worked in the shop caring for the business. All seemed well until about two weeks after my grandfather had departed. On that day I remember clearly the usual sounds of the early morning activity being different. I heard my father crying and my mother trying to comfort him. Later I learned that my father had dreamt my grandfather was dead. In the dream my father saw two of his brothers taking a plane to Italy to collect and bring back my grandfather's body. Later in the day a telegram arrived telling us that my grandfather had in fact died in his sleep that night.

At the age of nine this event did not seem strange. Both my parents appeared to accept the incident without ever questioning or exploring it in conversation. However, the incident stands out in my memory like a large red cherry placed among many white petals.

Even as very young children we have a well-developed view of what is real and what is imaginary. In tests where pre-school children were shown a ball rolled down a tube, the child expected the ball to emerge from the other end of the tube. When it didn't, the child walked or crawled to look behind the tube in an attempt to understand what had happened.

My father's dream had a similar effect. There was no external reason for the dream to occur. He had received no news from his father and no information to suggest his father was ill. Even if he had been worrying about him, why had he dreamt his father was dead? Two of his brothers did in fact take a plane to Italy to arrange for my grandfather's body to be flown back and buried in England. Why was my father's dream so detailed? How did he know the facts? Like the trick that conjured the ball away from the child's sight as it rolled down the tube, must there not have been some hidden mechanism behind the dream to produce the facts?

There are several ways of looking at such a coincidence. One is to believe that if we have enough marbles with two different patterns, one set with a circle and another set with a cross, mixing them together randomly will at times cause strange patterns to appear. In some cases a circle of crosses will appear. In others different recognisable geometric patterns will arise. Considering the billions of human beings in the world, and their incredible variety of activities, strange coincidences must result. But in such cases one would not expect *meaning* to arise as a part of the coincidence. My father's dream contained very accurate details. The pattern in mixed marbles would not reveal a person's future in clear images. Such random patterns would not bring a flood of realisation or a transcendent insight, as some coincidences do. They would not clearly synchronise an inner realisation with an exterior event. It is this synchronicity between inner and outer events that marks the divide between random coincidence and the sort of event that my father experienced and that I and my mother witnessed.

Another feature in the occurrence of coincidences is that they do not have to be an act of faith. There is no requirement for a particular belief system. Coincidences occur to the most critical cynic and materialist, as well as to those with devout beliefs in a supernatural life. If there is a hidden mechanism behind the event, it is certainly not firmly linked with beliefs or attitudes.

Our response to hearing a powerful coincidence described, however, will be very personal. Your own reaction to reading about my father's dream may fall within certain categories. You may have accepted it easily without questioning how it could happen. You may have accepted it with some thoughts about the principles that produced it. You may have rejected it in the belief that from the knowledge we have about the human mind and the world, such an event could not happen. You may even take the view that such experiences are works of the devil. Whatever your response, there may be more to learn about how, and perhaps even why, coincidences occur.

Caring – a key to the inexplicable

If we look at a few more coincidences we will have more material from which to extract understanding.

In 1978, Jaime Castell, a Spanish hotel executive, had a warning dream. In that year Jaime's wife had become pregnant, and the dream happened three months before the baby was due. In the dream a bodiless voice told Jaime that he would die before the baby was born. Although he was healthy, this impressed Jaime enough for him to take out an insurance policy against his death.

Not long after this, while driving on a motorway at 80 kph, Jaime was killed. A car travelling in the opposite direction at 160 kph hit the central barrier out of control and bounced on top of Jaime's car, killing both drivers instantly. The insurance payment was given without any suspicion. As a representative of the company said, 'This accident rules out suspicion … a second either way and he would have escaped.'[1]

Kath dreamt that a friend of hers who had been trying to become pregnant for nine years had conceived and was going to have a baby girl. When Kath next met her friend, she discovered she was pregnant. The friend did give birth to a baby girl.

Jaime wanted to care for his wife and future child even when faced by death. Because of the circumstances of the accident, there is no possibility of it being a self-fulfilling prophecy. I say this because it is a common criticism aimed at cases of premonition. Could Jaime's desire to care for his wife be a factor in producing his dream? It was certainly a factor in the way he responded to the knowledge the dream gave him, and the synchronous event that followed. As with my father's experience of synchronicity, Jaime found clear meaning in his dream.

A synchronous event of a different nature, and one that has been widely mentioned, involves two famous people. One was the film star Anthony Hopkins, and the other the novelist George Feifer. In 1971, while in London, Feifer loaned the proof copy of his novel *The Girl from Petrovka* to a friend. The copy was precious as it contained hours of work in correcting the book for an American edition. Within a week the friend told Feifer he had lost the manuscript. It had disappeared from the back of his car. Long searches and even the offer of a reward failed to locate the book.

Opening the door with need

In 1973, two years and two months later, Anthony Hopkins signed a contract to play in the film of the book. In order to better understand the script, Hopkins travelled to central London to buy a copy of the book. He failed to find one despite searching through many shops in Charing Cross Road, London's book district. While travelling home, Hopkins noticed something on one of the benches in Leicester Square underground station. At first he thought it might be a bomb left by the IRA, as they were active in London at the time. Daring to pick it up, he discovered it was the very book he was looking for. Hopkins later met Feifer while *The Girl from Petrovka* was being filmed in Vienna. Only then did the two pieces of the story fit together to uncover the amazing coincidences involved. In fact it was the proof copy Feifer had lost many months previously.[2]

The cases mentioned so far all have quite powerful factors involved. My father's dream informed him of his own father's death. A link with a parent, especially one on whom you have some dependency, usually involves deep feelings and needs. My father worked in a tool-making factory during the war, cycling fourteen miles a day to get to work and back. Working in his father's shop after the war was important to him. Were these the influences that opened some mysterious doorway to the dream?

Jaime Castell was a father-to-be. Insuring himself when he felt the possibility of death approaching was an act of care. Could it be that caring holds a clue as to why he had a dream warning him of his future?

Anthony Hopkins's experience is different in that it didn't involve death, appearing to link with the work he was doing, and the need he felt to pursue that work. Although in a very different category, the following coincidence also has a link with work and need.

Sandra and David shared the same work in the booking office of a UK company providing a cross-Channel ferry service. Attempting to use the fax machine, Sandra discovered it was not working. She tried to get it functioning, but when that failed she felt she ought to telephone David for help, even though it was his day off. Looking on the staff list, Sandra dialled what she thought was David's home number. When David answered the phone Sandra began to apologise and explain about the fax machine. But all David could say was, 'How did you find me?' He had been walking around the town of Dover shopping, and out of curiosity had answered a public booth phone that was ringing. On looking once more at the staff list, Sandra realised she had dialled David's staff payroll number.[3]

Thinking about Sandra and David's experience, one might still decide that with enough people ringing enough wrong numbers, something like this would happen eventually. The chances are very small, though, that David would be in exactly the right place at the very moment he could hear the phone ringing in a public phone booth, and that he would answer it. And what are the statistics of chance (in the Hopkins–Feifer case) in regard to a stolen book being found by the person who needed it and could tell the story to the person who lost it in a city of over eight million people?

> *PHONE NUMBERS*
>
> - A friend, Fred Townsend, tried to phone his brother-in-law, Peter Alexander. He dialled a wrong number, but didn't know, so wasn't surprised when Peter answered. But Peter was more than surprised, as he had been walking past a phone booth miles from home.
> - A man was just paying for some things he had bought in a sports store. The sales assistant was interrupted by a phone call. She looked at the man, puzzled. 'It's for you,' she said, looking at his name on his credit card. The caller had misdialled his office number and got through to the department store, surprising all of them.
> - Ken Anderson, while researching his book *Coincidences*, didn't have the phone number of a person who had reported a coincidence. Wanting to check the information, Ken rang directory enquiries and asked for the name and number. After a puzzled pause, the operator told him he was the person who had written to Ken.

Does this add up?

When Arthur Koestler was investigating synchronicity, Dr Tom Leonard, a professor of statistics at the University of Warwick in Coventry, wrote to him saying that any particular coincidental event has an infinitesimally small probability of occurring to a particular person. He suggested that in terms of probability, an unlikely event such as an 'extreme coincidence' has the likelihood of occurring to each individual at least once in their lifetime. Leonard tells the tale of a new professor of statistics who, in his first lecture, was describing the laws of probability. To illustrate this he took a coin out of his pocket and spun it into the air. Still turning, it fell to the polished floor of the lecture hall, continued to spin, then came to a standstill standing upright on its edge. The students applauded thunderously.

The mathematician Warren Weaver estimated that the odds against a perfectly round coin landing on its edge and remaining upright are in the order of 1,000,000,000 to 1. But Tom Leonard maintains that the upright coin was not a true coincidence, only a very unlikely probability. It would only be a coincidence if it happened again straight away.

Because of all the factors involved in such events as my father's dream, it is difficult to estimate the odds against it happening. We would need to know all the information my father held in his memory, the many things he had been told, as well as the enormous number of encounters with other people. In exploring this idea, Ken Anderson, writing in his book *Coincidences*, gives the example of a person dreaming that the Prime Minister is resigning. He says that if the following day the Prime Minister does in fact resign, the dream becomes a remembered and important event. But if the person has the dream and the Prime Minister does not resign, it does not become a significant event. In such cases we would not know the significance of such a dream unless we knew how many people dream about the Prime Minister's resignation in general. It is likely that such dreams occur regularly and have no connection with future events at all. So we are dealing here with probabilities rather than coincidences.

My son went on a school trip to Wells Cathedral. When he arrived back he told me he was in trouble. I didn't let him finish, but told him I knew exactly what he had done. I said to him: 'You have been playing around, and been naughty in the cathedral. I know exactly where you have been; you have been along a corridor on the left-hand side of the cathedral. You then went up some steps into a room. In the room there is a table, quite a long and very old table. The table was set up with place settings, with pewter, and everything laid out. You then went out of that room down some other stairs into the cathedral again.' My son could not believe that I had not been in the cathedral watching him. But in fact I had seen the whole episode in a dream while he was away.

Audrey B.

There are also other factors involved. My father never as a rule spoke about his dreams, so he was not a person who was regularly reporting them. Neither was he a man who generally showed his emotions. Therefore the dream he reported, and its impact, are outstanding.

What is the meaning?

Victor Mansfield, Professor of Physics and Astronomy at Colgate University, in his book *Synchronicity, Science, and Soul Making*, defines causality as 'one well-defined thing producing or effecting a change in another well-defined thing through the exchange of energy or information'. But coincidences usually have no clear causality. We cannot see the 'well-defined' things that produced the event. For instance, what 'caused' the connection between Jaime's dream and his fatal accident? Because of this, Mansfield particularly stresses the importance of meaning in connection with coincidences. The examples of my father's dream, and that of Jaime Castell, both have very pronounced meaning attached to the dreams. They both communicated very clear messages that were understood within the dream and in waking. Nevertheless it may impose too much limitation upon the subject if we stay with Mansfield's statement that meaning is always connected with a true coincidence or that there are no obvious causes. The following series of coincidences not only suggest events that do not carry some form of understanding with them, but also describe things that would be very difficult to call probabilities, or to assess statistically.

Outside normal experience

On 5 December 1664, a ship in the Menai Strait off the coast of North Wales sank with 81 passengers on board. Only one man survived. His name was Hugh Williams. In the year 1785, on the same date of 5 December, a ship with 60 passengers sank leaving only one survivor. His name was Hugh Williams. On 5 December 1860, a ship sank with 25 passengers. There was only one survivor. His name was Hugh Williams.[4]

The laws of probability may explain the survival of Hugh Williams in the first sinking. Stretching our imagination a little, we may describe the second sinking as coincidence. The third sinking on the same date and with the same named survivor stands in a category difficult to define. I think we might call this an anomaly. In different degrees each of the cases quoted has this quality of standing outside our usual experience of how things work. The psychiatrist Carl Jung said that such events are acausal. He meant by this that one well-defined event has not caused another well-defined event. The causes of such coincidental events remain hidden from us. There was no letter, no telegram, nobody making a phone call, no person telling my father that his father had died. Jaime Castell, through the usual channels of gaining information, had no way of knowing that a freak car accident would kill him.

An important doorway

At present science has no clear explanation for what Tom Leonard calls 'extreme coincidences'. Statistical analysis can assess to some degree what probability they have of occurring in a person's life, but this does not explain how or why extreme coincidences occur. This is not in itself a problem. Many things we accept as commonplace in today's world, such as electricity and heavier-than-air flight, were considered impossible or beyond explanation only a few years ago. When the earth was thought to be flat certain phenomena that were observed, such as ships slowly appearing over the horizon at sea, were also anomalies. They stood outside the understanding and possibility of explanation of the time. That some forms of coincidence occupy a similar position in respect to present-day science may simply mean that we have not yet understood the principles behind them. Of course, coincidences are not alone in standing beyond explanation by modern science. Life itself, along with consciousness, is still inexplicable. They are mysteries that remain well beyond our present understanding.

The aforementioned examples of the flat earth and heavier-than-air flight illustrate the possibilities that may exist within coincidences. Belief in a flat earth, for instance, set limitations to what people thought was possible. It also created great fear in approaching what were felt to be the boundaries of the earth. With a flat earth you might very well fall over the edge. Realisation that the earth was round opened up the enormous possibilities of exploration and expansion. A whole new age of travel, trade and discovery began. Similarly, with the discovery of heavier-than-air flight, not only was the world itself made smaller and in some ways changed, but people's lives were altered. Their expectations, beliefs and feelings as to what was possible, were enormously enlarged.

In a very real sense, the change from believing in a flat earth to recognising that the earth was round opened a doorway in the minds and hearts of people everywhere. The anomaly provided by a radical coincidence is just such a doorway for one's mind and heart. Even if in our examination of the subject we cannot be sure we have correctly explained it, the exercise of such an examination will start to remove the limitations, the fears and beliefs that portray a smaller world than the one open to us through the door of coincidence.

The analogy of a door is not a fanciful one. When we pass through a door, we usually move from one distinct setting into another. It may be that we move from a living room into a bathroom, or from the interior of our house to the environment of the street, or even from a dark room into light. Also, a door usually exists within some sort of structure or building; except in some modern art, it does not stand in the middle of a beach or a field.

The house your mind built

Although you cannot see it, your mind, along with your beliefs, has a particular structure or form. If the shape of your mind could be built into a three-dimensional model, such as a house, you would probably be able to see that it has as unique a shape as your fingerprints. But at the same time there would be features of your mental 'house' that were very much the same as for most of the people within your own culture. If there were a museum of the mind, it would be evident that the human mind has altered its shape in an evolutionary fashion just as the human body has. Mind models of even a few centuries ago would possess a much larger area devoted to religious feelings and thoughts. In the modern mind a much larger area would deal with personal identity. If these models in their three-dimensional format showed how we see and feel about the world, there would be a radical difference in the minds of individuals who were born after the discoveries and teachings of Galileo and Newton. Prior to their age, the world view was God-centred. It was a world in which human beings played an important role. After that period the universe came to be seen as a giant mechanism completely ordered by unbending natural laws.

It is uncommon to think of the mind being subject to evolution. Nevertheless this possibility is suggested by the historical events surrounding the emergence of modern scientific attitudes; particularly by the way they have influenced human beliefs and how we feel about our own identity and place in the world.

Looking at another case will help to make this clear. It comes from the near-death experiences of children studied and reported by Dr Melvin Morse, in his book *Closer to the Light*.[5]

Doctor Morse met Katie when her lifeless body was carried into the intensive care unit in which he worked. She had been found face-down in a YMCA swimming pool. Nobody knew how long she had been in the pool or what had caused her to become unconscious. Her brain was massively swollen. She had no gag reflex. An artificial lung machine was keeping her alive. She was one of the sickest children Dr Morse had cared for. He was sure she was going to die.

To obtain a reading of the oxygen in her blood, Dr Morse had to insert a catheter into one of her arteries. This was an unpleasant business and Morse suggested that her family, who were gathered around her bedside, might like to leave the room. Katie's father talked with his wife and the others, then asked if they could hold a prayer circle around her bed while the operation took place. They prayed aloud while Katie lay apparently lifeless, breathing only because of the machine.

Beyond time and space

Against all expectations, Katie made a full recovery. In an attempt to clarify whether Katie's drowning was caused by a seizure or an injury, Dr Morse had to interview her. When he asked this now healthy and bright seven-year-old what she could remember, she clearly recalled Dr Morse, and turning to her mother said, 'That's the one with the beard. First there was this tall doctor who didn't have a beard, and then he came in.' Katie went on to correctly describe the hospital rooms, telling how she was first taken to a large room and was then moved to a small room where she had X-rays. She accurately described details such as having 'a tube down my nose'.

Later, in another interview, Katie explained how, while she was apparently comatose and near to death, she not only witnessed what was happening to her sick body, but was also present in her family home watching what her parents, brothers and sisters were doing. She was able to describe the clothes they were wearing, food they were eating, and positions in the house. Her parents were shocked at the accuracy of her description. She explained to Dr Morse how she had met a woman called Elizabeth who was a guardian angel, caring for her while she stood between life and death. With Elizabeth she had met and played with two boys, Andy and Mark, who were waiting to be born. And then Elizabeth had taken her to meet what Katy called 'The Heavenly Father and Jesus'. When she was asked if she wanted to see her mother again and she said yes, she awoke once more in the body.

There are several synchronous events in Katie's experience. Although many people would describe her near-death experience as a vivid dream or hallucination, it coincided accurately not only with what occurred in the hospital, but also what happened at a distance in her family home. Vivid dreams do not exactly reflect external reality. However, the possibility of an internal 'imaginary' experience coinciding with external events does not fit many people's conception of how the world or the mind works. The mind structure in which many of us live – our mental house – has been built out of the materials provided by prevalent views that see the world ruled by immutable natural laws. These natural laws are defined as dictating that every event must have an observable physical or energetic cause. Such natural laws are said to determine that we have only one position in space at any one time. From this we believe – or rather are convinced of – a dualistic universe. It is one in which we exist independently of things other than ourselves. We have no connection with exterior objects or people other than through physically observable means. Because what happened to Katie does not fit this viewpoint, we may be tempted to consider it a fantasy or even a lie. That there are tens of thousands of such cases recorded may still not create a new window in our mental house that allows us a different view of life.

Although they were religious in the way of conventional Mormons, Katie's parents lived in a mental house that allowed no belief in the strange world revealed by Katie's experiences. But because they were so near to Katie, what they witnessed was akin to the sudden appearance of a door that had never previously existed in a wall of their house. Imagine that all through their life they had felt convinced that walking out of any exterior door in their house would lead into their garden. Then suddenly a door appears that leads into a completely different environment, governed by different rules. The rules of their ordinary mental house convincingly demonstrate that you cannot be in two places at once. The door that Katie opened convincingly demonstrated that you can. Through the new door there was also the possibility that death of the body was not the end of existence. Being in two places at once suggested an end to duality. Perhaps Katie was neither 'here' nor 'there' but in a condition we cannot 'see' through the usual doors of our mental house.

Is it one or the other?

This is not a philosophical point, but a practical and experiential one. Victor Mansfield reminds us of this by suggesting we look at the figure of the cube. When we look at the cube we either see it from above left, or from the front right. If you look at the cube long enough, it begins to switch from one view to the other. The point Mansfield makes is that we cannot see both views at once. The other scientific viewpoint arising from the work of Newton and Galileo suggests that this is a law of nature. Things are either one way or the other; they can never be both. However, in our own century it has been shown by precise experiments that this is not a fact of nature.

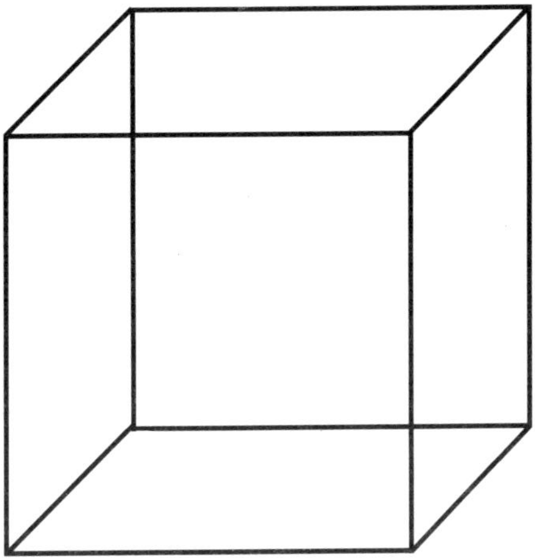

It is simply a limitation of our sense impressions and of the mental structure we have inherited or developed. This is important because the world revealed by coincidences gives us an alternate view, just as the illustration of the cube does. Neither view is incorrect. Yet often we maintain an attitude that only one explanation of the world and how it works is right, and anything describing it differently is wrong.

Mansfield carefully explains this point by describing what is currently understood regarding the nature of light. Classical physics considered light to be either a wave or a particle. Later detailed experiments revealed the paradoxical nature of light. It is both a wave and a particle; observed in one way it is a wave, observed in another way it is a particle. We can think of a particle as something similar to a small ball-bearing. A wave has the nature of ripples that we see on the surface of water.

The fact that light is both a wave and a particle is astonishing enough. More astonishing is the fact that its nature changes according to the way we observe it. Regarding this, Mansfield describes an experiment where one particle/wave is made to pass through a series of mirrors along different arms. A single particle/wave is called a photon. As the single photon passes through the series of mirrors, the method of observing it and measuring it is altered. This means that on its entry into the system the photon is a wave, but when the method of observing is changed, the photon becomes a particle. The astounding thing is that not only does it become a particle from that point on, but its nature is also changed in the past.[6]

This demonstrable fact faces our rational mind with a conundrum or paradox. To quote Mansfield: 'Now here is a real conceptual knot. It seems that our choice at the last possible moment determines what light did in the past.' Mansfield goes on to say that if we were to make the experiment more dramatic,

> Michael Talbot writes: 'Physicists have found compelling evidence that the only time electrons and other "quanta" manifest as particles is when we are looking at them. At all other times they behave as waves. This is as strange as owning a bowling ball that traces a single line down the lane while you are watching it, but leaves a wave pattern every time you blink your eyes.'

the true enormity of the findings would be illustrated. To do this he suggests that instead of thinking of light passing through mirrors, directing the light in different directions (arms), we should think of the light reaching us from the stars:

> Let the arms be billions of light years in length. Then we have a billion or so years between the interaction with the half-silvered mirror and the full-silvered mirror (used in the experiment). This means that my decision today affects what light did a billion years ago! This is too weird even for physicists, noted for their playful imagination, to contemplate. How could my decision today influence the universe billions of years ago?

Therefore, when examining the model of our mind, we need to leave space on one of the walls for a door. It needs to be a door that opens on to a different sort of universe from the one we may previously have felt to be solid reality. It is a universe that alters its appearance – no, its very nature – according to the way we observe it. Each question we ask of the universe, each attitude with which we approach it, each viewpoint we take, reveals to us a different universe. The universe is therefore not separated from us. We are intrinsically a part of it, and are participating in it. In some way the universe is constantly being created by ourselves as participants. It seems as likely, too, that we the participants are constantly being created by the universe. And the past is not set in concrete. In some mysterious way it is linked with what we do in the present.

We cannot yet claim that these revelations of science explain coincidences. However, they do point out that the universe is stranger than we previously believed. So the coincidences you experience or hear about may, hopefully, be an anomaly, opening a new door for you. It is a door that can reveal more of yourself, and more about the world around you. Coincidences are like the cartoon cat who runs to the edge of a precipice and carries on running without falling. Suddenly the rules of the world, which we are so sure are fundamental truths, are thrown into question. Like the worm-holes or the time-warps now common in films and television, coincidences allow us entrance into other dimensions of experience.[7]

BELL'S INEQUALITY THEOREM

Irish physicist John Stewart Bell put forward a quantum theorem that has revolutionised the way reality is considered. In brief, the theorem states that when two sub-microscopic particles are split and moved to a distance from each other, the action on, or of, particle 'A' is instantaneously reproduced with particle 'B'. This interaction does not rely on any known link or communication and is considered to stand above normal physical laws of nature, as it is faster than light. Prior to such findings it was thought nothing could transcend the speed of light.

Nick Herbert, in an interview published in *High Frontiers* writes: 'THERE ARE LOTS OF THINGS that are being kept from the public as far as the subjects of physics and consciousness are concerned. Bell's Theorem was proved in 1964, and it is still not taught in physics classes, and you don't hear it on your science news programs. A theorem is a proof, and no one has found a flaw in this theorem. It's such a simple proof that a high school kid can understand it. So physicists can understand it. They have various ways of trying to ignore it, but it can't be refuted because it's so simple.'

To quote Gary Zhukov: 'Quantum mechanics *is* the theory. It has explained everything from subatomic particles to transistors to stellar energy. It has never failed. It has no competition.'

The implications of the theorem are enormous. Something can be in two places at once. Apparently distant objects, or people, are intricately linked in an immediate way. There is no separate existence as we previously thought. Our view of the world is not one supported by the facts of physics. Time and space are transcended. David Bohm, an eminent physicist, goes as far as to say that all things in our observable universe are inextricably linked. Nothing has separate existence.

2
Walk on the Wild Side

Do you need science to tell you that the world you live in is extraordinary? Do you want quantum physics to prove to you that the environment around you is mysterious and amazing?

When he was a child, Steve Nicholls saw for himself that his life is a mystery. He says:

> When I was eight I remember vividly dreaming of coming down the stairs and entering the living room of my parents' house. Everything in the room was as it should be, as if I was awake. I could see the clock on the mantelpiece, and the time of the 'dream' was just past 11:00 p.m.
>
> We had a dog at the time and he was lying in front of the fireplace. My father was sitting in a chair reading a book. As I focused my attention on the dog, he raised his head and started whining. He then rose and began pawing the ground. I was convinced that I was in this room and not just dreaming, as I could see very clearly what was going on. There were none of the distortions or ambiguities that occur in normal dreams. After a few moments of the dog pawing and whining, my father told him to be quiet and turned to face me. I tried to speak to him, but he didn't appear to notice me. The 'dream' then ended and I woke up in bed, very confused and shocked. I was convinced that I had just been downstairs and could not see how I could have got back into bed with no recollection of climbing the stairs.
>
> The following morning I told my father about this and stated that I was very unhappy that he had looked right at me, but had not answered when I had tried to speak to him. He told me that I must have been dreaming and to think no more of it. However, a few years later, when I reminded him

> about the dream, he confessed that he had not wanted to frighten me, but that night he had seen the dog whining and pawing the ground, but he could find no reason for the dog's behaviour. There was no one else in the room at the time apart from himself.

Steve is just like you and me, an ordinary/extraordinary person. He is married to Sue. They have a child, and Steve works for a living, teaching guitar. His feet are on the ground and he pays his mortgage like the rest of us. Nevertheless the anomaly of coincidence has entered his life. His dream was not simply a night-time fantasy. What he experienced while asleep also had an exterior reality. He, like Katie, was in two places at once. His body, the locality of which we usually identify with our personality or consciousness, was in an upstairs bedroom asleep. But the awareness of himself was at the same time able to move about the house and witness distant events. But there was also another facet of this. The dog, and Steve's mobile awareness of himself, interacted. They were aware of each other. Doesn't that suggest a strange and astonishing world?

There is also information to be gathered from the reaction shown by Steve's father. He said he could find no reason for the dog's behaviour. Perhaps what he was really saying was that he could find no reason within his explanation of the world – or perhaps within the limitations of the world shown him by his physical senses. The dog obviously did not have these limitations. So it is interesting to speculate as to what the dog did use to see and respond to Steve. An autopsy on a dog does not reveal any strange or unusual sense organs. It has nothing more than we have. Indeed, we possess a larger brain. The fact that a dog can hear a wider range of sounds and experience a broader spectrum of smells does not explain how it sensed Steve's presence. If the presence of a disembodied personality could be measured by sensitivity to infra-red or ultraviolet, or by a greater awareness of smell, then humans would already have registered such presences on sensitive electronic equipment.

It is important, too, that Steve's dad used the word fear in connection with what he witnessed. Fear is probably very central to why we may live with a restricted view of the world. For some people their anxiety is so great that they cannot leave their house.

For others fear may explain why they stay in a damaging relationship: fear of change, fear of the unknown. In the first chapter I used the image of a house to represent the shape, the boundaries and the limitations of our mind. It is not only fear that may keep us locked within the walls and doors of our private mental house. Personal convictions that we already know the answers to life's mysteries can be equally imprisoning. Dr Richard Ash, a research scientist at the Carnegie Institution in Washington, DC, and Margaret Carruthers, of the Department of Earth and Planetary Sciences, American Museum of Natural History, sent me some interesting information about people's changing opinions concerning meteorites. According to Dr Ash:

> In ancient times and in many cultures it was quite accepted that rocks fell from the sky and there is much evidence that several Mediterranean cultures believed that meteorites were from the gods, and were venerated in temples and accorded much respect.
>
> With the coming of the Renaissance in Europe and the application of scientific method, it became increasingly obvious to 'men of learning' that the idea of rocks falling from the sky was quite absurd. After all, where could they possibly come from? Throughout the eighteenth century there were always scientists around who believed in the peasant tales of rocks falling from the sky, but they were in a minority and generally, because falls were usually witnessed by people out in the countryside (i.e. uneducated, 'unreliable' farm workers), they were poo-pooed.

In 1794 this changed because meteorites were seen to fall by 'reliable' witnesses. However, closed minds only open doors slowly. Not everyone was convinced. When a meteorite fell in Weston, Connecticut, in 1807 and the report of Professor Silliman and others was told to President Jefferson, he is apocryphally reported to have said, 'It is easier to believe that Yankee professors would lie, than stones would fall from heaven.' We could paraphrase this by saying, 'It is easier to believe a person would lie than to believe they could leave their sleeping body.'

Steve Nicholls is not alone in being able to have an out-of-body experience. It is not a strange phenomenon. Out-of-body experiences, or OBEs, have been reported by an immense number of people throughout history. Johann von Goethe, August Strindberg, D. H. Lawrence, Jack London and Aldous Huxley had or reported having OBEs. Dean Shiels, in studying 44 non-Western societies, discovered that only three do not believe in out-of-body experiences. Dr Robert Crookall collected enough modern cases to fill nine books. Celia Green, the director of the Institute of Psychophysical Research in Oxford, interviewed 115 students at Southampton University. Questioned about psychic experiences, 19 per cent of them reported having had an OBE. A larger survey of 380 Oxford students gave a higher percentage of 30 per cent who said they had experienced being out of the body. Most of these people stated that the experience was joyful, pushing back the boundaries of their beliefs.

Take this in! Feel it inside you. Look into the eyes of those you meet in a new way. You are much more than you have been led to believe!

> Your mind reaches far beyond the limited boundaries of your body and senses.
> Your awareness can exist separately or at distance from your body.
> You can relate to people or creatures you have no physical contact or link with. In this way you can know things about them or be an influence in their life even though you are far away.

Living as if …

In the tarot pack there is a major card called 'The Fool'. Perhaps it ought to be called the Wise Fool, because it depicts a man stepping over what appears to be a precipice. However, as he takes each step, previously unseen stepping-stones appear from nowhere. Coincidences are like this. We cannot see them coming, or where they come from, but they may often appear in our life at the most propitious moment. This is especially so if we live *as if* the bigger, more connected world revealed to us by coincidences were always visible and known.

In my twenties I was running a book business in my spare time, trying to circulate ideas that are now more fully a part of our mainstream culture. The books I sold dealt with information about diet, meditation and the human spirit. One of them was *There Is a River* by Thomas Sugrue. It is a remarkable book about the life of Edgar Cayce. It mentioned that although Cayce was dead, his work was being carried on by the Association for Research and Enlightenment – ARE. I was so moved and enthused by the contents that I wanted to find out what ARE were doing, and perhaps how I could help them. I therefore wrote to them asking for information about their activities and what books, if any, they published. I posted the letter but was not satisfied. So two days later I wrote again saying that I ran a book business, and if they wanted any help in this way, to let me know.

Len had been to Australia for seven years and had just returned to England. Deciding to buy an electric organ, Len went to Bath. On his way to the music shop he met an old friend whom he had not seen for seven years. When Len asked him what he was doing in Bath, the friend replied that he was selling an organ and was on his way to advertise it. Len bought the organ.

A week or so later two airmail letters arrived on the same day. The letter with the earlier date thanked me for my interest, enclosed information about ARE and asked whether I knew of a bookseller in the UK whom they might contact. A lecture tour of the UK was near at hand and they still had no one to handle their books. The second letter said something like, 'Hey, this is remarkable. The books are already on their way to you. Colonel Adams, the lecturer, will arrive soon. Keep on keeping on!'

Kevin Lowry tells a similar story connected with business:

> In 1997, I was travelling through London on business and decided to extend my stay another day so I could take in the pubs. The next day was Saturday and when I arrived at Heathrow to depart, I dreaded my decision because the weekend volume of travellers far exceeded the weekly norm. While waiting in an extended line to exchange my voucher for a new ticket, I heard a familiar voice behind me. Turning to see who was speaking, I was surprised to see my

> financial consultant and his family who were in the middle of a two-week holiday through Ireland and England. They had been scheduled to arrive in London two days earlier but had enjoyed Ireland so much that they extended their stay two days. Were it not for the coincidental timing, we would never have passed. What adds intrigue to this passing was that he had been trying for several weeks to get in touch with me before he left, but because I had changed home and work phone numbers, he was unable to reach me in a timely matter. Though we would have eventually connected, the prompt contact was important for financial reasons.

What happens in cases like this? Some writers on synchronicity state that a major coincidence is completely disconnected from a person's desire or wishes. This doesn't seem to apply to my own experience or to that of Kevin. His financial consultant had been trying to reach him for three weeks. An effort had been made through the usual channels to make contact, but had failed. My experience with ARE also involved efforts that had been made to find a bookseller in the UK. These attempts had failed. In both cases the extraordinary then took over and people who were trying to contact each other were brought together.

Perhaps I am over-simplifying this, but an image builds of people needing each other but through normal physical means being unable to make contact. Then, some other influence enters and people who perhaps have never met each other before are introduced. The following case illustrates this again:

> A BBC television reporter, who wishes to remain anonymous, travelled to America in order to gather information for a programme on ESP. At one point he needed to meet the project director of the Psychical Research Foundation in Durham, North Carolina – W. G. Roll. When the reporter telephoned Durham from New York to arrange a meeting, Roll's wife said her husband was so busy that it was unlikely they would be able to meet. So the reporter gave up on the meeting and took a flight to Florida to visit someone else.

> Amazingly Roll was on the same flight. This enabled them to have a long and easy talk, and the reporter got the information he needed.[8]

Living ***as if*** means that you accept the wonderful doorway that coincidences offer as an available part of your life. When you have tried to achieve something and failed, then you can confidently reach out to the invisible spirit infusing all life, and ask for your needs. Whenever you make a decision, especially a creative one, the moment you start to act on that decision, you involve the rest of creation, and hidden forces start responding to your action. The writer and philosopher Goethe wrote about this, saying:

> Concerning all acts of initiative and creation, there is one elementary truth, the ignorance of which kills countless ideas and splendid plans. The moment one definitely commits oneself, then Providence moves too. All manner of things occur to help one that would never otherwise have occurred, a whole stream of events issue from the decision, raising in one's favour all manner of unforeseen incidents and meetings and material assistance which no man could have dreamed would come. Whatever you do, or dream you can do, begin it. All this has genius, power, and magic in it. Begin it now.

Something pushes back

Shane Miller tells the amusing story of the little boy who took a pole to measure the depth of the pool at the bottom of his garden. Each day he measured it, and each day it seemed to show a different depth. He pondered on this, and one day found the thrilling answer. Rushing back to his parents he told them there is Someone, or Something, at the bottom of the pool, moving the stick up and down. The boy realises *he is not alone!*

Looking at coincidences, one may be forgiven for having the same enthusiastic and wondrous recognition as that boy. Dreams, too, reaching into the unseen and portraying it in images, show us something similar. In one such unforgettable dream, I stood before a shimmering and mysterious wall. The wall was like an upright body of water, as is portrayed so well in modern film effects. I reached my hand forward and tentatively pushed it into the shimmering wall. My hand disappeared into the mysterious substance. At the same time as my hand entered the wall, another hand, just as tentatively, reached out towards me.

> *COINCIDENCES ARE BUILT ON EARTH AND DELIVERED BY HEAVEN*
>
> - Can you ask for what you want? If not why not?
> - What first steps can you take to make what you want happen?
> - Have you asked for help?
> - Have you clarified your goals and decided exactly what you want?
> - What attitudes or fears are you putting in the way of receiving your desires?
> - Now is the time to take the helm of your ship of life and steer it in the direction you want to go. Ride with the tides, not as their flotsam.
> - Don't ask for anything except the best.
> - Create your opportunities by asking for them.
> - If you can't do it, learn how. There are plenty of people who will teach you.
> - Above all, remember that positive action calls upon the universe to be your partner.

This dream summed up for me the mystery of life in which we are all involved, and the one we confront in meeting coincidences. Because we are living it, life is always visible to us. Despite this, and at the same time, life, even our own personality, escapes final definition, and so remains invisible. As we extend our hopes, our need, our questing mind, or even our fear, into this unknown, so it reaches towards us. What comes out of that shimmering mystery is difficult to predict. But it does seem to depend in some way on what we extend into it. Of course what we extend does not simply relate to times of need, or times of purposeful examination. The tone of our life, our everyday actions and dealings with other people, are all extensions of ourselves into the world. The shimmering wall from which mysterious life extends towards us can be anything and everything. It can speak to us through the actions and meetings with animals or plants. We meet it in the people around us and what they say to us. We hear it singing to us or giving us information on the wireless or television. The sudden message, perhaps an all-important realisation, might confront us on a billboard. Nature itself, even through our own dreams and feelings, extends the mystery into our gaze.

Synchronicity of love

With this in mind, it is therefore interesting to examine how coincidence plays a part in meeting someone we can love and be loved by. When I met my wife Hyone, we were both participants in a group exploring spontaneous movement and sound. Part of the idea of the group was to give attention to what was arising in one's own body and feelings and allow this to express as movement and sound. I always found it quite easy to be centred upon what was happening to myself, and did not lose my attention to the sounds and movements of other people. On that particular day I did not experience much movement, but a persistent theme of speech arose. For a reason I did not understand, I kept repeating the words, 'Well, stop calling me'. I had many times previously experienced such spontaneous verbal expression, and had got used to the theme gradually developing until it became obvious how it related to my everyday life or psychological growth. But on this day the theme did not develop. Then suddenly I realised that what I was saying seemed to be interwoven with what someone else was saying in another part of the hall. It was a woman's voice, and she was saying, 'Leave me alone'. Each time she called this out, my own voice responded by saying, 'Well, stop calling me'.

This was a very strange experience. Both of us were married. It was the calling to each other across the room that made us aware of how we felt about one another. I have to stress that neither of us at first connected what we were separately saying with each other. The strangeness of the experience arose because when we realised the connection, we both felt as if some part of us had been communicating without our being aware of it. I consider this a coincidence because both of us were doing

> Betty, who had married Tom, dreamt that Tom had been engaged to a girl prior to meeting Betty. Tom had never mentioned such an engagement, but when Betty told him the dream he admitted it was true.

something we felt to be independent of anybody else. The link was provided by something other than our conscious mind.

Sometimes it seems as if the factors behind events in life go out of their way to bring us into contact with a particular person. Lee Baxter describes a fascinating series of events that led her to meet her dream husband. Her first marriage had ended in divorce. While dating another man, who was unsure about his feelings in the relationship, Lee was left alone on New Year's Eve, while the new man in her life went to a dance club. Feeling she was wasting her time waiting for him, and being the editor of a society column, she took her camera and went to local dances to photograph events. At the second venue a man asked Lee for a dance. He was on the way to getting drunk, but while dancing he asked Lee if she would invite the man he was with for a dance. He explained that the man, whose name was John, was blind. He went on to say that he had just met John, and to prevent him being alone on the New Year's Eve, he had persuaded John to come to the dance. Lee's mother had been blind, so she felt a special link with John. Also John had the face of a man she had dreamt would be her husband. Lee had been told by a psychic that 'a Father John will be very close to you'. When Lee walked up to John and asked him for a dance, he stood up and said, 'Old Father John isn't much of a dancer – but I'll try!' The dream and the psychic prediction were right. Lee and John became and still are close in marriage.[9]

The web of life

While researching this book and corresponding with a number of people about their experiences, many of them objected to the word 'coincidence'. For instance, Roseanne James wrote: 'Is there such a thing as coincidence, do you think? Or is there order and pattern in the universe? I seem to have encountered strange coincidences all my life, and I no longer believe they are random events, but are evidence of some larger design. Or perhaps even evidence of events, things, or people we are manifesting into our lives by our very desires.'

Nancy Staack expresses the same view, but in a slightly different way. She says: 'I believe there really are no coincidences in life. God is talking to us constantly – to show us the way, to ease our self-imposed troubles, to light our path – we just don't listen very well most of the time. He's fairly screaming at us, but we're surrounded by so much noise we can't hear. All we need do is just *be* and listen.'

On a similar theme, Toni Turnbaugh writes: 'I don't believe in coincidence, I believe a higher power is the key.'

Of course many people hold a totally opposing viewpoint. For them there is no mysterious link between individuals. No hidden process in nature links us one with another. There is only blind fate and unfortunate chance. Their argument is that we are all swept along by uncaring impersonal forces. We may be the victims or we may be the beneficiaries. Strangely enough, such arguments are often mixed with ideas such as the strongest or most ruthless will succeed. Or perhaps that only by personal effort or playing the game right can we achieve success, thereby suggesting the world responds to what we do. It is not, therefore, a game of chance.

In practical ways the concept of separation does not make sense. The clothes we wear, the food we eat, the house we live in and the materials it is made of, all arise out of collective skill, co-operative effort and knowledge. We exist in this collective creativity all the time. We depend upon it but perhaps seldom acknowledge it.

Even our mind is not wholly our own. The building block of self awareness and thinking – language – is not personally created. We inherited it ready-made by countless other people. Even our ideas and viewpoints are seldom unique to ourselves. Many of the things we do or strive for would be meaningless if there were not other people to share them with and respond to us. Our opinion of ourselves, our self-esteem, and our feeling of well-being are largely dependent upon relationships with other people.

Our connection with the environment is even more total. Without air we would die in a few minutes. Without fluid our death would take a little longer, perhaps a few days. Absence of food is the longest death; even so we are completely dependent on the plants and animals that are the basis of our food. And they, and therefore we, are dependent on the intricate web of living processes involving weather, water, soil nutrients, bacteria in the soil, insect pollination of plants – in fact the great web of life. We are all – humans, animals, insects and plants – totally connected with the energy of the sun and the substance of the earth. The sun is dying, and in its death pours out 90 per cent of the energy all living creatures on this earth need.

In a similar way the earth also dies as it gives up its energy and resources to living creatures.

As individuals the life that arises out of this constant streaming energy, not only from the sun and the earth, but also from other creatures that have lived, feeds our own pulsing life form.

Even so, the question confronting many people is whether all this connectivity is simply a chemical and biological accident. They might argue that such connectivity happened because it works. Meaningful coincidences question this viewpoint. Quantum physics, in demonstrating that two widely distant particles can immediately communicate, also punches a hole in the structure of the argument. If a simple particle can communicate beyond the speed of light, why not the consciousness of a human being?

While working with my friends John and Ann Clemence, who own the Capstone Hotel in Ilfracombe, Devon, I was helping to repair a flat roof on their house. The house is about a mile away from the hotel. As I was working on the roof, John told me that he was returning to the hotel. It had been a bitterly cold winter and John was gradually preparing for the coming season. Time passed as I worked and suddenly I heard John shout my name twice. This seemed strange as I had not heard him return. The tone of his voice was very urgent, so I climbed from the roof and looked for him. I could not find him in the garden, so looked through the house. He was nowhere to be seen. I stood puzzling over this for a few

INTERCONNECTEDNESS

David Bohm believes that our almost universal tendency to fragment the world and ignore the dynamic interconnectedness of all things is responsible for many of our problems, not only in science, but in our lives and our society as well.

For instance, we believe we can extract the valuable parts of the earth without affecting the whole. We believe it is possible to treat parts of our body and not be concerned with the whole. We believe we can deal with various problems in our society, such as crime, poverty, and drug addiction, without addressing the problems in our society as a whole, and so on.

Extract from *The Holographic Universe* by Michael Talbot.

moments when the telephone rang in the house. Answering it, I heard John excitedly shout my name twice; he had turned on the water mains in the hotel and discovered massive leaks due to frost damage. On discovering the leaks he had run from an upper floor to the telephone to get my help.

It seemed to me that John had mentally shouted my name as soon as he had seen the leaks. I heard that call over a mile away.

You and I be of one blood …

Whether we are a mother, a factory worker, a scientist, a business person, or a newborn baby, no matter how much we know, life is still a mystery. A university textbook on biology begins with a summary of what is understood in regard to living creatures. It ends the introduction by saying that despite all present knowledge we still confront the fact that life is a mystery. Despite thousands of years of human enquiry, despite hundreds of years of scientific investigation, life is still a mystery. It therefore ennobles us if we stand before this mystery with some humility. This humility might include the attitude that as we do not fully know what this mystery is, we cannot be definite about what it is not. If the coincidences that occur in your life, or that I have described in this book, reveal a little more of that mystery, stand before it with a glad heart.

The gladness might arise because the implications emerging from the few coincidences given are immense. They do not simply imply that we have psychic abilities, or that our consciousness can experience things at a distance from our body. Those are piddling little things compared with the major implications. If John's call reached me at a particular amplification, what is reaching and influencing me beneath my awareness? What is pouring out from my life and thought, and how is it influencing others around the world?

When I look at almost any row of houses, the attitudes of the people living in them are obvious from the condition of the house. One house will look flourishing and alive with plants, while the house next door appears devastated, the garden full of cans and rubbish. And that is only the surface, only the most physical and obvious of the creative and destructive influence we exert on our environment.

We all take part in creating the world. This creativity or devastation arises out of our attitudes, our emotions, our love or anger. Lynton K. Caldwell, in the book *Environmental Science*, writes:

> The environmental crisis is an outward manifestation of a crisis of mind and spirit. There could be no greater misconception of its meaning than to believe it is concerned only with endangered wildlife, human-made ugliness, and pollution. These are part of it, but more importantly, the crisis is concerned with the kind of creatures we are and what we must become in order to survive.[10]

The implications of coincidences point out that:

- You are an integral part of this planet.
- You are an integral part of the universe.
- Your mind is linked with the mind of others.
- You are a co-creator of the world around you.
- Your existence can never be separated from the existence of the universe. It is as ageless and as timeless as Creation.

This is not about politics. This is not about religion or weird beliefs. It is not about expecting other people to do for you what you can do for yourself. It is about recognising your dignity and place in the scheme of things and living your life from that joy.

Knowing your connection with things, you can dare to take creative chances, you can dare to stretch your wings and perhaps even fly. You can dare to walk on the wild side. For most of us, great coincidences do not happen frequently, but we can certainly increase them by living our life with zest.

If you doubt this is possible I want to remind you that the resources of the universe are standing off-stage waiting to be called. You may not understand fully what these resources are, but living with daring will call upon them more fully than hiding in a shell of separateness or anxiety. If you don't believe this, read what happens to these ordinary people when their resources are tapped:

> While at work one day in a large restaurant kitchen, I was cleaning a work surface during the lull before customers

> crowded in for their lunchtime break. About 12ft. away the boss, a man in his 60s, was talking to the head waitress Flo, a woman also in her 60s. They were conversing idly about the weather and how many customers were about for the season. Occasionally I glanced up at them from my work, but I was in no way trying to analyse them. Without any warning or apparent reason I could suddenly see both of them in a completely new way. It seemed to me as if a new sensory organ had opened, one I had never experienced before. With this new sense each tiny movement Flo and Boss made exploded with information. Subtle changes in a facial expression I had never perceived before were now visible and meaningful. It even seemed as if I could sense an enormous energy connection between the two. And what I understood through this new sense was that Flo and Boss at some time had engaged in sexual intercourse with each other. I was in my 30s at the time, and silly as it may seem, the idea that these two 60-year-olds could have sex with each other had never entered my mind. Along with this realisation came the vision of a great trunk of energy passing between them. Although on the surface their actions and speech were inconsequential, at the deeper level of energy exchange, very powerful communication was occurring. I saw that when two people have sex with each other they forge this link. Through it they send messages to each other perhaps without realising it. The link may last a lifetime.
>
> I was so surprised and intrigued by what had happened I asked Flo if she'd had a sexual relationship with Boss. With only slight embarrassment she said it was true, they did have a sexual relationship. She added that she would never look into my eyes again, suggesting I had some sort of psychic power. This was not true, I had never experienced such insight before, nor have I since.

We may be tempted, like Flo, to explain such accurate intuitions, coinciding as they do with reality, as arising from a psychic ability, or the intervention of spirits. This need not be the case. If, as Bohm suggests, we are at all times at-one with the universe, such insights are a natural part of our connection, unless we have barriers in the way. Such coincidences are therefore a normal part of our experience. This will be considered more fully in a later chapter.

The next example of walking on the wild side was described in Victor Mansfield's book *Synchronicity, Science, and Soul Making*. All the cases he includes are written anonymously at his request:

> Helen – I will give her that name – is a university lecturer. She was walking to the University and needed to cross a four-lane highway at an intersection. When the road was clear she started to walk across but without warning a car sped from a side turning. The vehicle hit Helen and she was thrown high into the air by the impact. As if in slow motion, Helen watched the woman in the car clutch her head in horror, as she watched the person she had hit bounce off the bonnet into the air. Helen, now in a timeless and transcendent awareness, was separated even from her own body. She watched the car below her pull to a halt. She could see her body hanging in space. She felt herself beyond danger, beyond time, existing in an eternal awareness.
>
> As the car stopped and the driver stepped out, Helen's body fell to the ground. As it did so she once more experienced life through her senses. Knocked completely out of her shoes by the impact, they were lying in another lane of traffic. The driver retrieved them for her, and with concern asked how she was. Strangely, apart from a small bruise on her little finger and left hip, Helen was shaken but unhurt. After exchanging information with the driver for the sake of insurance, Helen walked back to her house to report the accident. She later went to the University to teach a group critique in graduate art. Although unharmed, something had changed. She felt intense love for everybody around her. The exchanges between herself and her students felt inspired, and as if bathed in a flowing energy carried over from her moments in the transcendent timelessness. She felt it to be the most profound class she had ever taken.
>
> However, on returning home, a different reality caught up with her. Her critical mind began to tear the experience

> apart. Her out-of-body experience and her awareness of timelessness could easily have been the result of shock, and an attempt to avoid pain. As the beauty and love she had been experiencing was torn from her, she wept. She cried out, 'Oh please, please don't let me lose this!' At the moment of her cry there was a knock at the door. A woman Helen did not know explained that she wondered how Helen was, because she had witnessed the car accident. The woman went on to say that she had told all her friends at work because she had never seen anything like it before. When Helen asked what the woman meant, the woman said, 'Why, you went up in the air and didn't come down!'

This objective witness of her own experience was all Helen needed to renew the connection with the light and the love she had felt. She writes:

> My ordinary life was lifted above the physical laws that seem to govern it, and the door opened a crack to another reality. Now in my higher moments, there are occasions when my inner vision surfaces to pierce the mask of reality … My moment of transformation and breakthrough into an alternative self-awareness has indelibly changed my perception of myself in relation to the universe.

3
The Awe-Full Experience

While snorkelling off Atsitsa Bay on the Greek island of Skyros, I was cruising along in crystal-clear water about four or five metres deep. The water was warm and there were plenty of fish to watch. As I reached the tip of the island I suddenly swam over the edge of an underwater precipice. The water was so incredibly clear I could see into an immense depth, with thousands of fish adding dimension to the abyss. The sudden depth scared me, so I scrambled back to shallow water to gain confidence before once more floating over the abyss. It was an extraordinary experience, swimming in shafts of light, floating in enormous space in the midst of thousands of living creatures.

This describes, in a way, the feeling when we become aware of the immense web of life in which we exist. The analogy can be taken further, because one way of explaining how synchronous events work in our life is to say that we all float in an ocean of sentience.

The word 'sentient' is defined as 'having awareness through the senses'. But it also means or implies much more. Awareness allows us to respond to what is going on around us. Plants, for instance, respond to light. Their shape may radically change if the source of light is moved. Plants also react to pain or to subtle changes in the atmosphere – for instance, they close the petals of their flowers. Therefore we can say the plant is sentient.

We may feel, broadly speaking, that such ability to respond is confined to plants or bacteria. Yet the quantum experiments already mentioned, where a photon of light is one thing when observed, and something else when not observed, suggest that the fundamental particles of the material world can also respond. We can therefore think of them as being sentient. This is why I suggest we float in an ocean of sentience, one part of which knows, and perhaps responds, to what is happening to another part, even at a great distance.

Experiences such as my hearing John calling me from a mile away, mentioned in the last chapter, or certain OBEs, even imply that our mind is not in our body. Using the analogy of the ocean, we could say that the water that touches all life in the ocean is mind, and that our body and senses are a local awareness of that immense mind. Another way of putting it is that our mind resembles radio waves pervading all space. The radio signals are not in the radio, the radio is in the waves. The radio set only gives local expression to what is everywhere in space.

If we begin to become aware of that ocean of mind, then we have something of the feeling I had when swimming over the edge of the underwater precipice. Many people even feel anxious that they may lose their personality in the vastness. However, those who have dared to explore life within the great ocean of sentience, tell us that we are not swallowed up. Rather, we are cherished yet enlarged. Things to which we previously had no access are added to us. Our personal life becomes more obviously linked with the great web of life.

One day, while exploring a dream with my wife Hyone, I had an experience that helped me understand what it might be like to live more fully in the ocean of sentience. I don't know why it happened, but suddenly I felt the presence of two beings, the like of which I had never encountered before. They were not simply the spirits of people who had once lived, although in a way that is what I felt they were. They had lived, but now all that had been human was dead, so I felt I was meeting the living dead. This was slightly terrifying; not because the beings were threatening, or doing anything scary, but because I felt frightened that spiritual growth might take me beyond all human desire, all physical lust and longing, all personal ambition and grasping. In some strange paradoxical way these beings were totally dead as human people yet at the same time they were radiantly alive in a way I didn't fully understand. Through the death of all self desire, they had received a flowing radiant life that was universal.

Synchronistic experiences are a small radiance of that great universal life.

I am not alone

Sometimes we become deeply aware of being part of this huge sentient life. P. W. Martin, in his book *Experiment in Depth*, describes such an experience. While a soldier in World War One, Martin had marched with comrades all night in the pouring rain. Eventually they came upon a half-ruined village in the dark, and started to find places to sleep in barns and farm buildings. They were asleep as soon as their bodies touched the ground.

A shrieking explosion wrenched Martin out of sleep. A moment of silence, than another long, ghastly shriek and explosion followed as shells fell around them. Martin says:

> As I lay there on the floor, torn from the depths of sleep, I felt such extremity of fear as I had never known. From the waist downward I shook in an uncontrollable trembling, horrible to experience. In the same fraction of time, the upper part of me reached out instinctively, with a deep gasping breath, to something beyond my knowledge.
>
> I had the experience of being caught, as neatly and cleanly as a good fielder catches a ball. A sense of indescribable relief flowed through my whole being. I knew with a certainty, such as no other certainty could be, that I was secure. There was no assurance that I should not be blown to pieces in the next instant. I expected to be. But I knew that, though such might be my fate, it was not of great account. There was something in me that was indestructible. The trembling ceased and I was completely collected and calm. Another shell came and burst, but it had lost its terror.

Heather explains how she experiences awareness of her connection with the sentient web in a slightly different way:

> This has happened to me several times, and each time is similar. It is as though I have grown used to living in a room in a house. It is all I have ever known, so I take it that this is all there is of me. Then suddenly it feels as if the walls of that room melt away, or a door opens, and there I am stretching away forever. My mind, and what I can know, has

> no boundaries. If I think about a question, whatever it is, I have the most amazing response and insight, as if I have lived throughout all history. I feel as if I am part of a huge and unlimited sea of mind or consciousness. In it is all that has ever existed, merged and yet distinct. Every human talent and thought is in it, alive and vital. At those times I know with an unshakeable surety that we cannot help but be a part of this immense life. Yet at the same time we can be at odds with it, be unsympathetic to it. This causes a condition of stress within us, and within our relationship with it. But I feel that if we completely accept our place in this being, even though one is a minute and seemingly insignificant part of it, then we are aligned with its huge universal life and purpose. Then we become revivified in some way.

What Heather says about having a response from this huge sea of consciousness to any question she asked, is echoed by some people who have had a near-death experience. Dannion Brinkley, describing his own experience, says, 'I could ask any question and know the answer.'[11]

Edgar Cayce discovered, as an adult, that he could put himself at will into the state of mind in which he could tap this unconscious reservoir of knowledge. His work was supported by doctors because he could diagnose people's illness without examining them. He was also sought after by investigators of psychology and philosophy, and he dictated fourteen million words while in this state. His findings suggest that we all have this ability to tap the wealth of unconscious information – truly a collective unconscious – but few of us can bring it to waking awareness. His biography *There Is a River* is an astonishing and inspiring book to read.[12]

I am a child of the universe

If this connection is a fundamental part of everybody's life, then even the most insignificant events are part of the connection. Moreover, we and the universe are responding to each other. As an example of this, since starting to write this book, synchronous events are occurring far more frequently. In one weekend four coincidences occurred. I drove to another part of the country away from my home. A friend whom I had not been in contact with for months, and who lives in that area, tried to get in touch with me. His message was passed on, so we were able to meet and spend an afternoon together. One of my sons, who lives hundreds of miles away, was in the area at the time and I met him in the street. I wanted to meet a woman with whom I had corresponded, but felt I would not have time to call at her house. I met her as I was entering one shop and she was coming out of another. She confirmed what I wanted to know, that she had received a book I had sent. Finally, when visiting Brenda, my ex-wife, as I was leaving she suddenly mentioned an article she had read. I recognised this as having appeared in the edition of a magazine I had been searching for over many weeks. I was able to borrow the magazine to copy the article. Although none of these are major events, I nevertheless gained from them a sense of connection with the mystery that underlies my personal life.

> Robert had decided to take his girlfriend out to a meal, and knew exactly which pub he was going to. As he was driving there he put on a music cassette. However, his girlfriend said she didn't like it, and asked him where he had got it. He said a friend he knew about five or six years ago had given it to him. When they reached the pub, it was crowded and the car-park was full. Robert's girlfriend suggested finding somewhere else. So they drove on and stopped at the next pub they could find. The first person they met as they entered the pub was the friend who gave Robert the cassette.

Such events help us to begin looking beyond the usual limitations we surround ourselves with. We begin to recognise that Life, or the sentient universe, can communicate with us, or reach out to us in an immense variety of ways. We begin to see that not only are we receivers in this web of life, but we are also givers. Each and every part of the world around us is a mouth speaking to us, an eye seeing us, or a hand reaching out to us. Even the most inanimate objects can communicate something. Sheree, from Tasmania, describes such an event:

> A friend from overseas gave my Mum a little crystal. It has a suction cap and Mum stuck it on the window. It had been there ages but one day it flew off the window on to the floor a few feet away. Quite a distance. Mum thought nothing of it and put it back on the window. A few days later she received a letter from her friend's mother saying her daughter had died of cancer. Her death had occurred the same day the crystal popped off the window.

In his book *Man and His Symbols*, Carl Jung writes:

> It often seems that even inanimate objects co-operate with the unconscious in the arrangement of symbolic patterns. There are numerous well-authenticated stories of clocks stopping at the moment of their owner's death; one was the pendulum clock in the palace of Frederick the Great at Sans Souci, which stopped when the king died. Other common examples are those of a mirror that breaks, or a picture that falls, when a

THE HIDDEN LINK

Two books were recently published within months of each other. Both criticised the assumptions known as cognitive science. Both called for a more biological vision of the mind. They even shared a slogan: 'We must see the mind as "embodied"'. Other coincidences occur in the books *The Embodied Mind* and *Bright Air, Brilliant Fire*.

James Rusk, Jr., who writes under the pseudonym Harrison James, had no explanation when the kidnapping of Patricia Hearst in 1974, paralleled his book *Black Abductor* – later titled *Abduction*.

In 1898 Morgan Robertson wrote a book called *Futility*. Robertson had been a seaman, and the book he wrote was about a ship named the *Titan*. This had a displacement of 70,000 tons, was 800ft. long, had triple screw propulsion, speed of 24 to 25 knots, was designed to carry 3,000 people, and had only a few lifeboats. In the book the *Titan* hit an iceberg in the North Atlantic and went down. All these details were almost the same as the *Titanic*, which sank in April 1912.

> death occurs; or minor but unexplained breakages in a house where someone is passing through an emotional crisis. Even if sceptics refuse to credit such reports, stories of this kind are always cropping up, and this alone should serve as ample proof of their psychological importance.[13]

A case where a clock behaved in just this way comes from Winnipeg in Canada. The 72-year-old owner of a grandfather clock died, and the clock stopped at the exact moment of his death. It was given to repairers to mend but they couldn't find anything wrong with it. The family held the tradition that the clock should be passed down to the eldest son, but the man and his wife had only daughters, so his widow kept the clock. Then, on entering the house one day, she realised that the clock had somehow started running again. Minutes after seeing this, the telephone rang, and she was told her first grandson had been born a quarter of an hour previously. Was that a meaningless coincidence?

Everything is alive

In a sentient universe consciousness pervades all matter and space. Michael Talbot says:

> A material object, instead of being a 'thing' that exists separately from the universe, would be part of the interconnectedness of all things. It would be connected to the thoughts of every person who ever came in contact with it, connected to the consciousness that pervades every animal and object that was ever associated with its existence, connected via the implicate to its own past, and connected to the mind of the person holding it.

Gary Zukav, on a similar theme, gives an interesting argument for rocks and chemicals being able to respond. From our own experience we can see that metal responds when exposed to oxygen, forming rust. Even the most inanimate of objects changes when exposed to heat or cold. After giving other such examples, and mentioning recent findings in science, Zukav concludes that so-called inanimate objects are alive.

Whether or not we consider objects to have some form of sentience, there is sometimes a strange relationship between objects and people. Carl Jung tells the story of a German mother who took a photograph of her small son just before the outbreak of World War One. While in Strasbourg, a French city near the German border, she took the film to be processed. The start of the war stopped her from collecting the film. In Frankfurt, two years later, she gave birth to a daughter and purchased a film to photograph the baby. The film, on being processed, was seen to be double exposed. Her young son and her new daughter were both on the film.

Reading such experiences, we may respond to them as interesting curiosities. Yes, it *is* strange that a mother used the same film she started to use two years before. It *is* curious that a clock stopped when its owner died. Merely to regard these examples as providing a few moments of entertainment, is, I believe, to be neglecting something magnificent. We are missing something that can touch us with awe and meaning. We have overlooked a grand connection between our most intimate self and the rest of the world. Perhaps we have lost sight of the bigger picture, the overview that allows us to see what part synchronous events play in our own life, or in the lives of others. Phil Cousineau helps us to understand this by describing one such event in his life.

He tells us that at the end of the 1970s, after a week of heavy house painting, he went to his favourite secondhand bookshop in San Francisco. Browsing for an hour, Cousineau was drawn to a copy of *Two Years Before the Mast*, by Richard Henry Dana. As a newcomer to San Francisco, he found the book fascinating because of its description of the Bay Area just before the city was founded. He read until dawn, marking passages, and lost in the descriptions of the California Indians and the cruelty of life aboard ship. Cousineau worked all the next day painting, still full of the images described in the book. When he arrived home late that evening, a small package lay on his doorstep. It was from his father, with whom he had never felt closely associated because of their differences. Inside the package was a copy of *Two Years Before the Mast*. It was the same edition and in the same condition as the copy Cousineau had purchased. A note from his father suggested that the book would give him a background to his new life in the Bay Area, and he had listed his three favourite scenes in the book. They were exactly the same ones that had captured Cousineau's own imagination. Cousineau says:

> I was struck with nothing less than a sense of wonder. Moreover, the peculiar convergence made me feel connected to my father in a way I hadn't been for years, or at least aware of the connection that had been there all along. The incident defied explanation, but more importantly helped me focus on my relationship with my father in a way that is at the heart of the mystery of synchronicity. A mirror had suddenly been placed in front of me, and everything in my life seemed altered.

His father, when told about the coincidence, was at first sceptical. Then as Cousineau explained the details, the bond that had opened through the event deepened. A sense of the indescribable beauty and symmetry of life flowered in him. Cousineau ends his description by saying that his father continued to send the 'right books at the right time' for the rest of his life.[14]

The wonderful invisible

Looking at coincidences in this way helps us to move beyond the idea of them being mechanical actions in a strange universe. The coincidences that Cousineau described not only opened doorways to a fuller relationship with his father, they also revealed the hidden connections that his everyday actions had with others. Within them was a learning experience giving him a different view of life and of his place in it. This enlarged view of life and one's hidden connection with others is beautifully described by Dr Morse.

A woman who lived in New York travelled all the way to Seattle for a consultation with Dr Morse. She told him: 'It has been 1041 days since my son died. I have not slept more than four hours a night since then.' Morse felt a feeling in the pit of his stomach, remembering his own five healthy children. He sensed that he had nothing to offer this woman in her loss. The woman showed him a picture of her son and began to speak of him, but Morse was called from his embarrassment due to an emergency with a critically ill newborn child. Leaving the mother in his office, Morse hurried to the hospital, only to find the baby was already recovering. As he wrote up the notes for the case, a nurse who had been helping asked, 'Who was that who came in with you? Is he a student?' Morse did not understand what the nurse was talking about as nobody had come into the hospital with him. As he was trying to find a pen for the notes he was writing, he pulled out the photograph of the woman's son. Immediately the nurse said, 'That's him. He kept trying to get your attention.'

When he returned to his office, not having the courage to tell the mother that a nurse had apparently seen her dead son, Morse asked her if she had ever been contacted by her son after his death. She said, 'Oh yes. After he died, for several nights he would stand at the foot of my bed and tell me he was alright, and that I should stop crying. But that was only a crazy dream, it was just something I wanted to believe. It seemed real, but it couldn't have been real.' Hearing this, Morse suggested the woman should use simple relaxation techniques to turn off the inner critic robbing her of the contact she had with her son. In his own words:

> She should then ask her son for help in healing her grief. I asked her to write down everything she dreamed about, and her first thoughts on awakening, and take her journal to a grief counsellor in her home town. The mother wrote to me later, and told me that was the first night she had slept well since her son died. After years of going to various grief workshops and psychics and mediums, she learned the seeds of her own healing were right at the foot of her bed.[15]

Stand back and see the beauty

If we think of coincidences in the narrow sense of countless marbles making strange patterns, we miss the beauty and change touching that mother. That the nurse's experience of seeing the woman's dead son was synchronous with her desperation in seeking help, is more than a mechanical juxtaposition of events. I don't believe we can separate what happened from the mother's love for her son, Dr Morse's pain that he couldn't help her, and – if we accept that her son has survived death – then his love and care for her. They are all important factors in the total event. And what part did the nurse play that she had such clear vision, and drew Dr Morse's attention to what she saw?

The overall effect of such cases suggests not only that the processes of life synchronise events, but also that the universe is friendly. Unfortunately, most of the time we have too much of a close-up view of events to see this. We are too near things. For instance, if we judge our life only from what is happening today, or even this week, we will have a very different view of it than if we could see it from a span of 20 or 40 years. Similarly, our home town, when viewed from the ground, looks very different than when seen from the air. From high in the air, or from space, we have a more global and connected view of things. Instead of seeing only a small part of something, such as a house or a street, we can see all of it, and how one part connects with another. With human events, our smallness of vision does not allow us to see what repercussions occur, not only in the life of the recipient of a big synchronistic event, but also in the lives of those around them. We may also be blind to what effect any particular event has on the future.

When we look at the case Dr Morse describes, we are also seeing only a small part of what happened. To understand this we need to think not only of the moving event of the mother being reconciled to the death of her son; we must also remember the countless cases where such help and reconciliation does not occur. Why do amazingly synchronous events happen to some people, or at some time, and not to others? If the universe is friendly, as some of these cases suggest, why is there so much tragedy? Why isn't there more intervention to support and help us?

Coincidences, in fact, come in a multitude of forms. Most of them go unremarked. I heard recently that a male acquaintance, while working as an engineer on a road, was hit in the head by a dislodged cat's-eye (a reflective glass road signal used in the UK). It had been thrown up by a passing car. A fraction of a second's difference, a slightly different position in space, would have totally changed the result. Why was that man in exactly the right position, at exactly the right moment, to receive that blow to the head? Unfortunately he was seriously injured and is crippled mentally by the damage.

Can we call such an event an accident? Wouldn't it be better to call it a synchronistic event? That man's movements and decisions had placed him at that exact point to be injured. This is not to suggest that he deserved to be injured. It is only an attempt at better defining a situation. I make this distinction because some coincidences lead us to wonder if words like accident and mishap are over-simplifications. Only with a more global view could we begin properly to understand what is involved in destructive or supportive synchronistic events. In this context, one often hears the cry that if there were a God in heaven, such things would not be allowed. This is a strange criticism, because if our lives were so ordered that we all went around doing good to one another, it would mean we had no free will. As many parents know, when children reach the age when they start making their own decisions, awful things can sometimes happen.

What would the world look like if we did have a more global view? How would we examine the painful or disastrous events in our own life from that perspective? Some years ago I met a woman who, after a love affair that suddenly ended, experienced a slowing down of her mind. She said it felt as if time and her thoughts stopped. In that condition her awareness expanded, taking in vast areas of experience she had never dreamt of before. She saw her life, and the lives of those around her, from a completely new perspective. At the time, the war with Vietnam was in full swing. In her usual awareness she felt the war to be pointless and a human tragedy. From her enlarged viewpoint, standing beyond birth and death, she saw that things were as they should be. All the events in the world and in her life were the working out of things that we human beings had put into operation.

Of course, what she says is a huge generalisation. Nevertheless one can hear similar statements from other people who have experienced what Dr Richard Bucke called 'Cosmic Consciousness'.[16] Such people assure us that what we take to be tragedies in our life only appear as such because our limited local awareness sees death as an end, and life events disconnected from their causes. They tell us that the problems or even tragedies in our life are the means to learn important lessons and skills, in a journey that is eternal, not restricted to the small span of our physical life.

Life transforming light

Whatever the truth of this, there is something important to learn from Dr Morse's study of the children who lived to tell of their near-death experiences. Many years after his first interview with them, he returned to see what, if any, effect the experience had left in their life. He says that eight years after his original study of the Seattle patients he decided to re-interview them. He wanted to find out, as they had grown into adulthood, what these people – who had talked with beings who glowed with an inner light, and who had stood beyond death – were now like. To quote Dr Morse:

> I found that these children have become special teenagers who have excellent relationships with their families. They share a maturity and wisdom that is humbling. This group from the Seattle study displays a conspicuous absence of drug abuse and even experimentation. They exhibit little rebellion against authority, no excessive risk taking, and no teenage pregnancies. These people were selected for the study because they had survived cardiac arrest. Yet instead of the brain damage and retardation that usually result from such a traumatic event, they had good grades and fine behaviour. I spoke to each and every child from the original study and found these traits in all of them.

Although Dr Morse started his study as a sideline, thinking he would prove there was some physiological or chemical cause for the near-death experience, his viewpoints and his own life were changed. He sums it up by saying:

> All these years later, I accept what the ancients knew: all men must die and death is not to be feared. There is a Light that we will all experience after death, and that Light represents joy, peace, and unconditional love. These children

> have taught me that we each have the ability to experience the Light and that the Light teaches us that we are all important in our own way.

Few of us may have the wonder of a near-death experience. But I believe that each of us can open the door to a meaningful coincidence. Perhaps we will not talk with an angel, but we will be touched by the splendour and mystery of life.

4
The Wonderful Humdrum Existence

When the psychiatrist R. D. Laing was using LSD as a psychotherapeutic tool, on a few occasions I was invited to his consulting rooms in Harley Street to observe. Because of my long work with unconscious tensions and the part dreams played in their release, I was fascinated by what LSD revealed of the unconscious. I had read a great deal about the drug's use in helping people deal with neurosis and other physiological or human problems. So when, on two occasions, Laing offered me the chance to experience the drug myself, I said yes.

Some of the things that happened, for instance an enormously heightened occurrence of synchronicity, are particularly relevant to the subject we are exploring. But one of the events has remained a beacon of understanding, shining its light across the 30 years that have passed. It happened during the first session. I needed to go to the toilet to urinate. It was a great pleasure to do this, and to watch the falling water splash into the pool, creating many bubbles. But something caught my attention, for it seemed that each small bubble was an eye looking up at me. Wondering what this could mean I looked more closely, to see not eyes, but I's. Each bubble had a tiny reflection of myself in it. Because the drug amplifies the ability of our waking consciousness to receive information from the unconscious, I was led to see each of the tiny replicas of myself as having separate identity. The suggestion behind this was that I, and everybody else, with our personal identity, are like bubbles. We are all in our own sphere of skin, apparently separated, and yet at the same time, all part of the same substance. As this interesting line of experience developed, I saw that each of the separate bubbles had awareness only out of my own consciousness. They were all unknowingly reflections of me.[17]

Suddenly, and with some fear, I realised the meaning of this interesting fantasy. I am a bubble. My personal awareness, although it seems distinct and separate, is in fact the reflection of one great consciousness pervading the universe. So who am I when my bubble bursts, as it must, and I return to my source? The fear I first felt has long melted. It has been replaced by joy as I have explored what it means to burst and return home.

My exploration has led me to believe that one great consciousness pervades everything. That is why I have said the universe is sentient. Of course many people before me have been lucky enough to experience the same thing from ancient times. As it says in the Bible, 'Lift up the stone and there shalt thou find me: Cleave the wood, and I am there.[18] And in Matthew: 'I say to you, as long as you did it not to one of these least, neither did you do it to me.'[19]

William Blake says it beautifully:

To see a World in a Grain of Sand
And a Heaven in a Wild Flower,
Hold Infinity in the palm of your hand
And Eternity in an hour.

The extraordinary is in the ordinary. The transcendent is in the common. The apparently far-off and unreachable is here with you at every moment. The holy is the person next to you – you yourself. Aren't these the messages coincidences send to us? Can you see in the beautiful, the strange, and the far-out synchronous experiences, notes of music from the symphony of a sentient universe?

In this symphony of synchronicity, where one instrument harmonises in time with another, even though they are of different shape and make different sounds, the most ordinary is touched by mystery. This is because life continually responds and communicates with us through everything around us.

Roseanne James told me that she was dithering about moving house, even though she had put it up for sale:

> I really need to get out of this place because I have no life here, and have never really fitted in with the local culture. West Wales, however, has a much more New Age ethos, and

LOST AND FOUND

- A young man took a book on psychology from his local library. He read half of it, then lost interest. A couple of days later a friend of his sister found the same titled book in a busy street. Hearing that he was interested in psychology, she sent it back via his sister.
- A nun of the Good Samaritan order in Sydney saw a man lying ill in a car park. She only had a $5 note in her purse, but called a cab to take the man to hospital. Later that day while parking her car, a starling hovered over the bonnet. It dropped a piece of paper it had been holding. On picking it up, the nun discovered it was a $5 note.
- Boone Aiken lost his engraved fountain pen in Florence, South Carolina in 1953. In 1956 he was in New York City with his wife. As they left their hotel, she saw a pen on the ground. It was the pen he had lost. His name was inscribed in two places.
- While fishing in a Norwegian fjord in 1979, Robert Johansen caught a large cod. He gave it to his grandmother for a family meal. When Thekia Aanen gutted it, she found the diamond ring she had lost while fishing in the fjord ten years earlier.

a sort of hippy-dippyness about it (which is much more me), and as such I would be able to make more friends and do the sort of things that I never seem to be able to do around here. My oldest and most barking friend also lives down there, and I could meet people through her. Well, anyway, to get to the point: I drove down there a couple of months ago, and as I was driving out of Carmarthen to head towards Llandyssul, I was thinking about this move and wondering if it was a good idea. Ahead of me I suddenly noticed a rainbow (which has always been significant for me) and at the very same moment from the stereo in the car I heard Neil Finn (from Crowded House) singing: 'It's something written in the sky …'!

We are all dancing to the rhythm of life, even if we can't hear the music. Again and again I have been talking over something important with my wife, and at that very moment the words of a song echo the thought on the radio or television. But it isn't just other people singing or talking who are the messengers; objects also are part of the music. Sandy S. explains an experience illustrating this:

> I had visited a therapist in London and was wide open from the experience. Emotionally I felt like a child, yet I had to travel back to the West Country where I lived. Getting to Paddington Station was difficult, but when I got into a carriage full of people, I began to lose hope that I could stay in control. To make matters worse, a very motherly woman was sitting opposite. I felt sure she knew I was scared stiff of bursting into tears. I dared not look at her because she appeared so sympathetic I would probably have fallen forward into her arms.
>
> As the train pulled away I sat tense and fraught, wondering if I would make it. The track goes through tunnels for some time. Every so often, however, there were large vents open to the sky. As I sat almost gritting my teeth, we moved into one of these vents. Brilliant sunshine shone full on a massive billboard. On it were two words – TAKE COURAGE.
>
> The impact on me was incredible. It felt like a personal message from God. I knew I was going to make it – not just on the train journey, but on my longer life journey.[20]

Although such events may appear random and, at the best, fortuitous, looking at coincidences as a whole, evidence suggests they are part of patterns, cycles and mathematical connections our life has with the sentient web of life.

Alan Vaughan, after investigating prophetic dreams surrounding the assassination of President Kennedy, noticed that synchronistic events in the lives of past presidents seemed to recur in the present. From this study he predicted in November of 1968 that 'enormous scandals in the Nixon administration will come to light, probably in the second half of his administration'. Then, in 1976 Vaughan predicted that Jimmy Carter would be elected. Vaughan says that his reason for publishing such predictions was to show that 'the underlying blueprints of life have a scientific validity'. As science claims, when we can correctly predict an outcome, it is because the underlying laws of the phenomenon are understood.[21]

Working with the whole

That we are part of a whole does not need argument. It is obvious that we are part of the process of life, and that without the interaction of other parts we would have no food, no drink, no air, no clothes, and so on. What is arguable is whether there is an integrity in the wholeness. In other words, the billions of your body cells, each with their own tiny life and action, somehow manage to integrate into a conscious personality you know as yourself. Does the whole organic process of our world, or the cosmos, have a similar focus of awareness arising from its parts? Is the sum greater than the parts, as the saying suggests?

If, through the action of coincidence, you can glimpse this greater whole acting in your life, then it seems wise to find some way to work with the wholeness, rather than against it.

Over a period of 30 years, my work has been involved with exploring the unconscious. Working with spontaneous physical mime, with fantasy and especially with dreams, I explored, not only as a teacher and a therapist, but also in my own life, how the unconscious emerged into personal awareness. I have worked hard at defining how areas of our experience, that have not been previously clarified or formulated into words or concepts, become conscious or known. Many things in our life are sensed through impressions gathered over a long period of time, or from innumerable separate events.

It is obvious to me from these years of experience and work, that we all have a sense, even if poorly defined, of the sum of our experience being greater than the parts. Most people have never worked with their unconscious mental processes to define this impression. Nevertheless it may still emerge to some extent in the form of dream images or fantasy. My experience of being a bubble, described at the beginning of this chapter, is an excellent example. As with most realisations of this nature, it suggested that my individual life was given existence by something that was underlying all other living beings. It also clearly says that the sum behind the parts has awareness. I had never previously been confronted so directly by this perception of myself. That is why it contained an element of fear.

Obviously I am not the first to discover this. Carl Jung gave this greater awareness the name of the Self. Most cultures in the past believed that a transcendental reality underlies our personal life and the universe. This idea of the universe responding to us has already been mentioned in the previous chapters. I state it here again simply because of its enormous importance, and because this relationship needs further definition and description. Getting near to such an enormous reality may at first be frightening. Roseanne James, describing her meeting with the transcendent, says:

> I have reached that state so many times now. It's as if you are standing on the edge of something, and all you have to do is let go, and you will expand out in all directions, and become the actual universe ... a point of consciousness, but everything, all at the same time. But, I cannot let go ... I want to, but it terrifies me as well ...

Therefore, working *with* your wholeness instead of out-of-phase with it may need some personal growth or adjustment. The advantages, however, are so great in terms of finding personal meaning in your life, meeting a loving life partner, contacting people who are helpful in work or life, and getting what you need, that being at odds with your wholeness is not the most creative option.

Many years after my bubble experience I used a technique called the Lucid Waking Dream to explore the question of who I am if my bubble bursts. In other words, what is my underlying wholeness? The technique uses a form of deep relaxation to enter a dream-like state. From that condition you allow your unconscious to spontaneously express, but you can watch the process without being asleep.[22] Here is my description of what happened:

> I had a waking dream in which I lived in a world in which there was a huge multinational organisation or 'company'.

> The company influenced everything and everybody. I appeared to be about sixteen, approaching manhood, and facing the question of whether to join the company or not.
>
> My feelings at first were that if I did I would be another cog in the huge machinery of its massive workings. I felt threatened by this, as if I would lose my identity. But the organisation would not go away simply because I tried to ignore it. It was everywhere and in everything, so where was there to hide? This led me to feel ready to join. Still feeling a bit threatened I met the manager – not God – but someone experienced in the place. He welcomed me and assured me that there was going to be no attempt to take away my identity as Tony. In fact it would be useful to the organisation if I continued to live and work in my accustomed manner. The only change would be that I was given a gadget like a bleeper. It represented intuition. Through intuition I could link with the Whole – the united being of the organisation of Life. This link would guide, not control, my individual activities to help them harmonise with the overall working of Life. This felt wonderful and so simple and clear. Behind the smallness of my personal being lay the immensity of Life, of which I was a linked part, living my individual life yet working with the whole.

Coincidences are ways we experience our personal connection with the whole. To quote Phil Cousineau:

> In this sense, an experience of synchronicity is a soul moment. It is an electrifying experience, as sudden as a visitation by a god, a palpable inrush of grace and power, one of the defining moments in life, a sudden conviction that we might move beyond fate and realise a hint of our destiny.

This electrifying experience, this grace, this working with the Whole, is obvious in the experience of Dr Lawrence Le Shan. He is a psychologist who has written about parapsychology, mysticism and meditation. A description of this coincidence appeared in *The International Journal of Parapsychology*.[23]

Early in December of 1967 Le Shan sent a manuscript on mysticism to Dr Nina Ridenour. She is a psychologist who specialises in mental health, but also is a well-known expert on mysticism. Later, in December of that year, Le Shan and Dr Ridenour met to talk over the manuscript. As he respected her judgement, Le Shan took notes of her comments. In particular, she said his manuscript suffered from his lack of knowledge regarding mysticism, and she suggested a number of books he should read. She mentioned one book, Bing's *Vision of Asia*, saying, 'Until you read this, you won't understand the difference between Eastern and Western mysticism.' This was an impressive statement as the difference was crucial to what Le Shan had been trying to cover in the manuscript. So he went straight from the interview to the Library of Parapsychology to see if they had the book. They didn't, so he went on to the Library of the Theological Seminary, again without success.

Hurrying home late that evening, on impulse Le Shan walked a slightly different route to normal. The traffic lights were against his crossing at one point. As he stood waiting for the lights to change, his attention was drawn to a rubbish bin near the crossing. Next to it, lying on the ground, was a book. He idly picked it up. The title was *The Vision of Asia*, and the author Cranmer-Bing.

But that isn't the end of the story. On phoning Dr Ridenour the next morning to tell her the strange tale of how he had found the book, she asked which one. On telling her she said, 'I have never heard of it.' She affirmed not only that she had never heard of the book, but that she hadn't mentioned anything like it to Le Shan. So if it wasn't Dr Ridenour's voice talking to Le Shan about the book, one can assume it was Le Shan's own intuition. And if he was hearing the voice of his own Wholeness, it was obviously interested in the work he was doing and lending a hand!

Where have we heard a story like this before? Wasn't it Anthony Hopkins and *The Girl From Petrovka*? And this help with work we have seen in Kevin Lowry's experience of coincidentally meeting his financial adviser, and in my own synchronous offering of my services of a bookseller to the company who were seeking one. Sometimes, however, the guidance we get, the web of coincidences involved, is creative in a much greater way. At times of remarkable creativity, the conspiring of events, people, information and action are remarkable.

Creativity breeds coincidence

Mike Tanner, a long-time friend, recently reminded me of coincidences surrounding what turned out to be a wonderful joint creativity. Mike writes:

> You and I bought our houses in Woodlands, Combe Martin, within a month of each other. At that time I was in a situation where I had nobody expecting me to do anything and was able to look at different viewpoints. You had a huge collection of books that you fed me. I started working with the Samaritans and met Shelagh Johns. She asked me about yoga. Which led me to introduce her to you as you were teaching it at the time.
>
> I happened to be with her at New Year's Eve, and at midnight I put on a bit of music from Holst's *Planet Suite*. I had a Samaritan client staying with me – unusual – and Shelagh was designated to befriend her. In the new year, when Shelagh was visiting the client, I bumped into her and she mentioned that she was going to see you afterwards. I said that I would come along since I hadn't seen you for a while. When we arrived you said, 'Oh Mike's come too.' Unbeknown to myself Shelagh had arranged to have a session with you. I agreed to join in, and as we walked up the stairs you were humming or whistling the same piece of music that I had played on New Year's Eve!

What Mike describes are peripheral coincidences leading to what then happened with Shelagh, Mike and myself. The 'session' Mike mentioned was an experimental group exploring how to find healing from the internal conflicts and traumas we all hold in ourselves. In effect it was about how to reach towards wholeness. Within two weeks a way of working had emerged that none of us had in any way defined prior to our small group getting together. We called it The Seed Group.[24] It was a way of working therapeutically with a small peer group, and was later used by other group leaders. At the same time another incredible process broke loose in the group that became Self-Regulation (SR).[25]

The discovery of the Seed Group was for me one of my most creative acts, and one that became a major part of my work for over 20 years. I can see that without the involvement of two very special people, Mike and Shelagh, what happened would not have been possible. I have met a lot of people in my life, but not many who would stick with me, for no payment, through seven years of challenging exploration as we delved into what the Seed Group and SR were capable of. So the creative event was many-times-over a combination of coincidences, a great synchronous harmony.

But even this is still too much of a close-up view. We are still looking at events and people over a period of only a few weeks or months. Even though, in terms of world events, the creative act that happened was quite small, it still has enormous links with the past and future. The attitudes with which we each approached the experimental group had arisen out of the many years of our lives. The information we each held in memory had been gathered from a multitude of people, either through relationship, through the media or reading. All of these many strands were the material from which the situation was woven in which the creative act could happen. And then, what arose in each of us from experiencing the Seed Group passed on into the lives of hundreds of other people. The links, and the inter-connections, are beyond understanding. In fact each case of coincidence we have looked at has this wider picture, if only we could see it. The glimpses people have of this wider picture are what we generally call a 'spiritual experience'. Our life as it would appear if we could see all its interconnections, all its received and given influences, is our spiritual life.

The force is with you in business

When we stand in front of an old-style upright piano and sing a note, the taut strings of the piano vibrate and sing the note back to us. If we sing a different note, the strings also sing differently. The living world around us constantly responds to us like the piano strings.

Whatever we think or do, life sings back to us, or responds in harmony. The songs and harmonics that life sings to us are what we experience as our everyday life and its events. Occasionally something out of the ordinary happens, and this we call a synchronous event, or coincidence.

While I was living in the Jericho area of Oxford, near the canal, I stood one spring day on a bridge watching the ducks with their tiny newborn chicks. Although they were only fragile balls of fluff, the chicks were swimming, each one of them sending ripples out over the water from each small movement they made. These ripples interacted with the ripples coming from the other chicks and the adult ducks, actually moving the chicks up and down. I also saw that when a bird is swimming, then stops, the ripples carry on moving through the space or medium of the water – on and on. I don't know why, but it impressed me that a point in space where the bird had not moved was filled with the ripples it created somewhere else. Suddenly, with a thrill of realisation, I saw that each of us is sending out such ripples through our voice and movements. We radiate ripples of thought and emotion. The marks we leave in the world, whether as a painting, a mother's love, a business, or a smile, are centres of energy rippling out into the world. These ripples reach far beyond our body. They continue long after physical death. Perhaps they are the basis of our spiritual existence, the observable part of us that lives on.

What ripples out from us, of course, is not simply our conscious feelings, but our whole unconscious disposition, with whatever love, guilt, anger we have within us. I had an extraordinary experience of this at a time when I was feeling frustrated with my work situation. I had given many years to study and research in the area of dreams, along with practical use with individuals and groups. I felt that my abilities were not being used. At the time, I came across the sentence in the New Testament, Matthew 18:19. It reads, 'Again I say to you, that if two of you shall consent upon earth, concerning anything whatsoever they shall ask, it shall be done to them by my Father who is in heaven.'

I took this to mean that if two people could stand before life with a good heart, and make a request, it would be given. I remember at the time it seemed important to be very clear about what I wanted. With my wife Hyone's help, I defined it as follows:

- I wanted work that used my abilities.
- I needed reasonable pay.
- The work should involve some public acclaim, as this was a personal need.
- The work should not stand in the way of the time spent with my family.

Hyone and I spoke this request aloud with sincere feelings. The next morning, being out of work at the time, I was painting the front of our house. The telephone rang while I was up the ladder. It was our local post office telling me that a telegram had arrived for me. It was from the national newspaper, the *Daily Mail*, asking me to telephone them. When I did so they offered me the job of dream columnist for the newspaper. The work fulfilled every part of my request.

When I later asked the editor how it was I had been picked for the work, he told me his search had led him to telephone Marshall Cavendish, the publishers of build-up encyclopaedias. I had worked with Marshall Cavendish some years before on a dream feature. They had in turn chosen me for that feature because of my book on dreams published in the 1970s. So the link had been formed by events stretching into the distant past. But how had it happened the day after our request?

If you have begun to see that you are connected to all other beings, and that the universe responds to you, then you have the answer to the question. When you accept this, your business activities, your creativity, especially when it is risk-taking, will be enhanced by synchronistic events. Marjorie Kelly, the founder of *Business Ethics* magazine, describes an experience of her own which illustrates this. With her partner she had been putting together a business plan to launch a publication. It was to be a project expressing things they felt passionate about. They estimated the launch cost would be $14,500. As this would require asking other people for funds, they decided to think it over, but maintained their enthusiasm to create the new publication.

On arriving home, Marjorie received a phone call from her brother. It was to ask her if she had received her inheritance cheque. Picking up the pile of waiting letters, she opened the one containing the cheque. There in her hand was a cheque for $14,500.

Because business confronts us with many important risks, because we chance our own and other people's money, because commerce is deeply involved in other people's lives through work opportunity and product, it is a creative furnace for synchronicity. Tamas Makray, who founded Promon, a project management company dealing with electronic engineering, described synchronicity as an 'extraordinary set of circumstances, lasting only for a short time, like opening a window, giving opportunities for development'.

Jessica Satori, herself an entrepreneur, and the author of *Synchronicity – The Entrepreneur's Edge*, describes coincidence in business as 'unexpectedly meeting people, collaborators, customers, partners, at the time of decisions or options'. With many business people who describe their experiences of synchronicity, the opportunities or openings, the people met, do not occur because the individuals seeking such opportunities have waited passively. As with Marjorie Kelly, they have carefully defined what they want, and considered what they need to get it. As happened when I defined my own needs for work, they often get exactly what they have asked for.

If you are in business, however, or if your life centres around some form of creativity, it is not enough for synchronous events to happen to yourself. They must also happen to other people. It is other people who respond to your product or art. The person who goes into a store looking for a particular item and who finds it on the shelves has had an experience of a coincidence. This may not be as impressive as Le Shan finding the copy of *The Vision of Asia*, in the case already quoted, but it is still an example of a wish being fulfilled.

So, in working with synchronicity in business, it has to be recognised that almost 100 per cent of the business action takes place outside of the awareness of the company owners or staff. In fact, most of the action in our individual lives also occurs beyond our awareness. This can be seen in the example I gave of the work offered me by the *Daily Mail*. The conversation between the editor of the *Daily Mail* and the staff of Marshall Cavendish was completely outside of my awareness, even though it deeply influenced my life. In a similar way the tens of thousands of my books circulated throughout the world may be the subject of conversations I will never know about. Even so, in some measure they influence my life through the sales of my books.

This hidden life is a vital part of our existence. Most of it remains hidden to us. Occasionally, however, through coincidences, we catch a glimpse of this mysterious process. It is a glimpse into how our individual life, or our business endeavour, is totally interwoven into the lives of other people. Kathy Gardarian, who started the business Qualis International, manufacturing recycled plastic bags, had a startling experience of this. She was in the office of a buyer, who was disagreeing with her about a programme of sales she was suggesting. The buyer didn't think the programme would work. He was telling her this when his telephone rang. The caller was the president of the company. The president didn't know Kathy was sitting in the buyer's office. He told the buyer that he particularly liked Kathy's programme. The whole meeting then swung around to a more positive note.

Buckminster Fuller, in moving away from the brink of suicide, and after a year of deep self interrogation, realised that if he worked always for others and only for all humanity, he would be optimally effective. He went on to design the Dymaxion House, that was capable of being mass-produced. This was at a time (1927) when there was a housing shortage in the US. He had harnessed the power of that hidden action. If you are loved/liked/wanted enough, then other people will do the work for you.

But sometimes a coincidence appears to arise from an even more mysterious source

HELP IS NEAR AT HAND

Bel Geddes only had $5.83 left when he sat in a park and noticed a magazine lying next to him. Flicking through the magazine, he noticed an article saying that the millionaire Otto Kahn thought the rich should help artists. Bel immediately spent most of his $5.83, sending a telegram to Kahn explaining his desire to produce plays and design sets. Kahn wired Bel $400. With this help Bel went to New York and got a job designing opera sets. He gradually worked up to become one of Broadway's best designers, and a famous designer of car bodies and household goods.

than the action of other people. Jane Taylor, a skilled illustrator of religious books, tells of such an incident:

> A few weeks ago I was sleeping when I got what I can only describe as a 'mental e-mail'! It was very fast – just the words 'North Devon Journal, Cartoonist', and that was it. But it stayed with me when I awoke, and so, being short of work, I considered the idea, and decided our local paper really did need a cartoon strip to liven it up! So I rang the Journal and spoke to the editor's secretary who said, 'Oh, we advertised the job last week and we've had 60 applicants. In fact the closing date has passed, but if you can get some samples in today I'll put them in the pack with the others, because the editor hasn't had time to look at any of them yet!'
>
> This was the first I had heard of any cartoonist job being advertised – and I later learned there were applicants from as far away as Newcastle! I took some samples of my work in, and was subsequently shortlisted. The end result is that six artists have been asked to do a sample strip for the paper and one of us will get the job!

Jane went on to question whether this was a coincidence or a 'sixth sense'. The intuition was certainly coincidental with the advertised job. But it was an intuitive awareness that motivated Jane in the first place. Being a Christian who believes in spiritual guidance, Jane tries to remain open in a prayerful way. This openness to the action of life from within us, and from outside us, appears to be an essential part of working alongside the mysterious power of synchronicity. That, and the clear asking for what we want, will be looked at more fully in a later chapter.

As I was finishing this book, Jane wrote to say:

> Just thought you would be interested to hear of the outcome to my dream (North Devon Journal Cartoons etc). I received a phone call today informing me that I am now their official cartoonist. So I got the job!!!! Apart from £40 per week, I'm not too sure what the cosmic significance of this is, but I thought I would let you know.

The well of understanding

In the New Testament, John 4:7, the story is told of the woman from Samaria who went to Jacob's well to draw water. There she met Christ who told her many details of her life, and said that if she asked, she would be given the living waters of eternal life. Hearing these things, she went to the city of Samaria, and told the people there, 'Come, see a man, which told me all things that ever I did: is not this the Christ?'

Was Christ psychic? Did he have strange abilities that enabled him to look into a person's past? Or is the story expressing itself in symbols, and thus saying the best in us can stand near a fount of inspiration and intuition, uniting us with the living waters of life?

While attending a three-day intensive meditation course, something wonderful happened to me. Perhaps the technique exhausted my thinking mind, because suddenly all thoughts ceased. This in itself is an amazing experience. Most of us have never stepped outside of our thinking and feeling. The perceptions our thoughts and feelings give us are taken as personal reality. Like the old story of the fish taken out of water, we may never know we exist in this element until thoughts stop. When this happened I experienced self-existent consciousness. Usually events and stimuli call forth our thoughts and feelings, which are constantly moving and shifting with the events and stimuli that produce them. But self-existent consciousness doesn't move. It has no cause outside itself. It just is. In that condition I stood in the Garden of Eden, a garden that is here and now, not in the past or far off. I mean by this that I had a completely different perception of time and the world. I was no longer separated from the plants and animals around me, but was aware of them being part of the spectrum of my life, and they of mine. We all shared in the exquisite and timeless moment of creation – now. Only my own self-interested thoughts and motives had cast me out of this wonderful garden.

While in that state, a woman asked me a question to which I replied by telling her something that had happened to her an hour before. I later walked through a room in which a woman was resting and started singing a song. Only afterwards did I learn that my answer to the question was deeply perceptive, and that the woman in the room had been thinking about her father, and that the song was his favourite. Was I psychic? Or was I, at that time, experiencing the wonder of the eternal waters flowing through me?

I am convinced that we each stand by that well. From it we can draw inspiration, wisdom and healing from an infinite source. This has nothing to do with being psychic, or having strange powers. It has everything to do with opening our heart to the wider life of which we are an integral part. I am convinced of this because of things that have happened to me. One experience stands out as a

> Brian Westlake told me: Some years ago I ran a junior football club for under twelves. One day we were getting ready for a game, and just before kick-off one of the boys, Kevin Jenkins, came up to me and said, 'Brian, your car's suspension has gone. It's all down on one side.' I went straight to my car, but it was perfectly okay. But as Kevin didn't have an explanation why, I thought he had been winding me up.
>
> Two weeks later, at another game, my daughter attended the match, the first time ever, and just before the game she came up to me and said, 'Dad, your car's suspension has gone. It's down on one side.' I said, 'Hey, what is this, you're just winding me up.' She said, 'No, come and look.' When I looked, the car was on one side, the suspension had gone. The garage told me they had never seen a suspension in such a bad way. It could have gone at any time. So I wonder if somehow Kevin was warning me. A little while later I loaned my car to my brother. While driving it on a motorway he smelled petrol, and quickly got his wife and children out. Just in time as the car burst into flames.

perfect example. I was teaching in Greece on the island of Skyros, at the Atsitsa holiday community. At the communal lunch one day I was telling some of the people sitting near me how I had been helping my son Neal write a book about hand-reading. Some of the people naturally extended their hands for me to tell them about themselves. I explained that I knew nothing about the subject, as Neal was the expert. But I did tell them what each line was said to mean. As lunch ended, a woman – I will call her Beth – who had been listening asked me if I would look at her hand. I had to rush off to teach, but said I would sit with her soon.

An opportunity came about two days later, so we sat in the sunshine and I looked at Beth's hand in the way I had with the other people. All I could tell her were trite things about the lines on her hand. I had no conscious awareness that she was in distress, and she had told me nothing about herself, but I felt dissatisfied with what I had said. I therefore closed my eyes and opened to the loving life and wisdom we are all part of. Immediately I had a very strong sense of two things. The first was that something had brought a great and unwelcome change into Beth's life. The second was strange and moving. I saw a picture of Beth sitting alone in her home, reading. But behind her was a man trying to get her attention and tell her of his love and care for her. Unfortunately Beth could not see or hear him, as he was dead.

I told Beth about the change I felt had occurred. She then told me that not long ago her husband had an affair with another woman and it had completely altered the direction of life in a way she didn't want. We talked about this for a while and then I asked her about the man standing behind her. I described the scene to her again, telling of his death and continuing love and support. She broke into deep sobbing as her pain at last found release. She explained through her tears that when her husband took the other woman as her lover, the woman's husband had become Beth's friend. The friendship had moved on to them also becoming lovers, and this love had helped her through the dark months of her pain. But six weeks ago he had died and she missed him terribly. The message of him standing nearby gave her strength.

I was as amazed by this event as was Beth. Where did the information come from? I have tried since then to do the same thing, but little happens – at least, when I try a scientific experiment to see if it works. Yet occasionally a similar response comes when someone asks for help out of real need, or there is a crisis. Therefore I conclude that I, as an individual, do not have any power of insight. But when there is real need, or someone cries out for help – not to me, but to life – then a response from life can come, transcending my own inadequacies. Then I, or anyone with an open heart, can be a voice or agent for that wider love and life.

Each of the examples I have described has a synchronous quality. At the time of singing or saying them, I had no idea how, or if, they connected with the people I was talking with or near to. The fact of their synchronicity only became known afterwards. This suggests that many of the things we do, when we are open to wholeness, connect with people in a way beyond our understanding. Perhaps we only become aware of the significance of a tiny proportion of these events.

Carl Jung warned that we should not believe we have power to bring about a synchronistic event. This would be akin, he says, to the ancient witchdoctor, who believed that through a magic ritual he could cause an eclipse of the sun to occur. I have no argument with this. Meaningful coincidences are as much a part of natural events as a thunderstorm. However, the argument that synchronicity is a natural event, beyond human will to influence, takes a stance suggesting that as human beings we are somehow outside of nature. This is strangely at odds with the latest theories of physics. In their mildest forms, these theories show we are participating in the events of nature. Our simple observation of an event can change it. In their most radical form, these theories, voiced by people such as Bohm, say that we are each an inseparable and integral part of a whole. If this is so – and the personal experiences of the many people quoted suggest it is – what we each feel and think, what we long for or are hurt by, is felt collectively by life itself.[26] This is so fundamental that it is strange there is argument about it. We know that what we do individually and collectively has changed the face of our planet. If this were not so there would be no concern about global warming. But perhaps the argument is about how our individual attitudes and actions might call a response from what has been regarded as a mechanical, non-sentient, universe.

The centre of the argument seems to be whether we, as living forms, are hermetically sealed units, having no links with one another apart from sound, sight and touch. This would mean that we are like small ball-bearings, each having separate existence, and only influencing each other through bumping. But what about magnetism? What about the fact that tiny electrons can communicate one with another faster than the speed of light, over enormous distances? This suggests otherwise. That sub-atomic particles change their fundamental nature when observed by a human being also suggests a form of sentience at this primal level. However, to argue about these things, other than as enjoyable speculation, is ridiculous. Neither science nor individuals have arrived at a theoretical model of the universe that forever remains unchanged. As Wilder Penfield, the father of neurosurgery, wrote after a lifetime of investigating the human brain and mind:

> Whether there is such a thing as communication between man and God, and whether energy can come to the mind of man from an outside source after his death is for each individual to decide for himself. Science has no such answers.[27]

Drawing upon the waters of life

Our ability to stand by the well, and receive the waters of life, can be improved. Peter Fenwick, Consultant Neuropsychiatrist at the Maudsley Hospital, the foremost psychiatric teaching hospital in the UK, and President of the British branch of IANDS (The International Association for Near-Death Studies), says that 47 per cent of people who have a near-death experience report an increase in their psychic ability. Sheila Freeman, after a cardiac arrest during an operation said:

> A very important aftermath was that it has left me with a sort of heightened awareness. Everything creative, like art, music, literature, also people, animals and nature seem almost too beautiful, touching or vulnerable – I get such a deep emotional response, sometimes it seems almost unbearable.

Of course we do not need to have a near-death experience to become more aware of the information the universe shares with us. Alan Vaughan has an interesting perspective on this, when he says:

> Consciousness is Creator, and the sum total of all consciousness is the ultimate Creator. Psychic phenomena and meaningful coincidence are the very demonstration that consciousness lies outside space and time – and indeed creates them – as it creates our lives.

Similarly, Edgar Cayce, who appeared to be capable of communicating with the cosmic mind at will, taught that extended awareness is our birthright.[28] What holds us from it is that we do not open to the wider life. Our personal desires and fears limit our horizon. By acknowledging that we are an important part of a living and conscious universe, our boundaries begin to thin, allowing life to touch us, and speak to us, more easily.

Our wholeness can communicate with us in almost any manner. It can come in a dream, as with the mother who dreamt her son was in danger. She knew he was travelling in connection with his work, but had no telephone number to call him. So she knelt and prayed for his safety. At just that time he was asleep in a hotel room and was wakened by hearing his mother call him. He then realised the hotel was on fire and managed to escape before being harmed.

It can come as spontaneous movements, expressing or miming something our conscious mind is not flexible enough to receive. In these cases, it feels as though our body is being moved without our conscious will. Last night, while driving back from a visit to the gym, I heard a man describing this on the radio. He was in hospital waiting for a kidney transplant. His pain was excruciating and he was certain he was dying. For no reason he could understand, his hands wanted to move and paint. As soon as he took hold of a piece of paper and allowed his hands to paint spontaneously, his pain receded. If he put the paper down, the pain returned. In his own words:

> It felt as if Him up there was moving my hands. I had never experienced anything like this before. It was so wonderful I thought maybe this was how Michelangelo and the other great painters felt all the time – as if they were being guided. But it had never happened to me until that time. Then a kidney was found and the transplant took place. Through the pain a new door opened for me, and I've had ten years of being able to paint.

The communication can come as a child telling us what's in its heart, or as a bodiless voice speaking to us, or as a sudden deep sense of conviction. However it comes to us, it brings help for our own spiritual growth, for our everyday affairs, and for the uplift, support and healing of others.

The miracle of parenthood

Becoming a parent is one of the most wonderful events that can happen to anybody. Fame, riches, creativity in the arts, pale into insignificance when measured against the miracle of the emergence of a new life. Even if our child is born with some form of handicap, life is still a miracle. Many of us can paint, or write a song. Many can gather extraordinary riches, or move millions of people with artistry. But no one, out of their own skill and knowledge, can create a child. In such immense creativity we must become partners with the mystery of life. We must stand in that mystery and witness the wonder that is conception and pregnancy. We are only workers in the vineyard as the new child emerges into its growth.

For many people, conception, pregnancy and birth have many synchronistic facets connected with them. For instance, while practising a new form of meditation, I saw what could almost be described as a mental slide show. Without any obvious links with what I had been thinking beforehand, I suddenly saw the mental image of a friend, Janice's daughter. This was strange because it was almost as if the image had intruded into my flow of thoughts and feelings. I therefore held myself open to see what, if anything, came next. In the same manner, there was a sudden shift and the image of a baby arose, just like a slide projector with a new photo. I asked the mental question as to whether this meant that Ella, the friend's daughter, was pregnant. The slide changed again and this time the baby was obviously a boy, with a crown on his head. About two weeks later I had reason to phone Janice, and at the end of dealing with the business behind my call, I asked her if Ella was pregnant. She laughed, without replying. When I asked her why, she said she didn't know if Ella was pregnant because she had just gone to find out that afternoon. It turned out that Ella was pregnant, and she did give birth to a boy.

The thousands of near-death, and out-of body, experiences now on record from around the world not only begin to give evidence for continuing life after the death of our body. They also show the possibility of existence before birth. The experience of Katie, who was drowned in the YMCA swimming pool, is an example. During the time her body lay lifeless, kept alive only by the machine breathing for her, she described seeing not only what her family were doing, but also meeting and playing with Andy and Mark, two boys waiting to be born.

My experience with the image of Ella's unborn baby boy had a similar quality. It was a soul waiting to be born to Ella and her husband.

Conception and birth are, quite by themselves, enormously synchronistic events. A baby is born at a particular time of day, in a particular time of year, in a particular place on earth, in a particular country and culture, to particular parents, in a particular period of history, leading up to particular future events. This is often thought of as of no importance, but when you collect enough cases of coincidental events, you begin to see that dates and even places frequently have powerful connections in the life of that individual. Toni Turnbaugh told me:

> In our family we seem to have birthdays and important days, anniversaries, etc., on the same day of the month, same month and day in some cases. For example, I met my husband on the 21 January, the same day as my younger brother's birthday. My husband's birthday is the same day as my sister's, 11 March. My mother was also born on the 11th day. My brother Brian's birthday is the same day as my grandmother's, 8 February. Both sets of grandparents were born on the same days of the month, 8th and 13th. My birthday is also on the 13th day and I'm left-handed. My grandfather's birthday is also the 13th and he is the only other person in the family who is left-handed. My oldest brother Michael was born 30 July. My firstborn, same day, 30 July. My son was born on 17 September, my boss's birthday. Why I am not sure, but I could probably go on and on.

Anna Murray, a BBC researcher, told me:

> In our family things always happen on the 17th of the month. I was born on 17 June. My mum's mother was born on 17 July. She also died on 17 July. I got my degree results

> on the 17th. I graduated on the 17th and I also got together with my better half on the 17th. In our family everything seems to happen on the 17th. Not only that, but three members of my family live in houses with the No. 17.

I have no explanation as to why such clusters occur in some people's life, except that life is fundamentally a great linked web of interactions. But our birth may tie in with usually overlooked forces, other than those represented by dates. Intrigued by this question, Ken Anderson[29] looked up the birth dates of people who had succeeded in life. He discovered that a disproportionately large number of US congressmen – 42 out of 620 – were born on Christmas Day. Checking further, he found that 600 out of the 9000 people listed in *Who's Who* were also born on 25 December. He estimates that is fifteen times above what it should be.

Edgar Cayce, the great psychic from Virginia Beach, was able apparently to speak from a state of expanded awareness. When asked about the origins of life, he summed it up by saying:

DATES AND NUMBERS

- Successful clergy are four times more likely to have been born on 25 December than on any other day.
- The actress Ingrid Bergman was born on 29 August 1915. She died on 29 August 1982.
- In the town of Ardenes in Norway, the Henriksen's have three children, Heidi, born 1960, Olav, 1964, and Lief-Martin, 1968. They were all born on 29 February.
- Mr Rhea was born on 5/5/55. He was the fifth child. The family address was No. 5. His present address is at No. 5 and his clocking-on card at work is No. 5.
- Howard Trent's address, in Fresno, California, ends with 742. So does his telephone and bank account numbers. A cheque for compensation he received after being in hospital was 99742, which matched the last numbers of his telephone number. Tyres he bought had a serial number ending in 742 and the licence plate on his car is FDC742 .

> The cosmos was built with the tools which man calls music, arithmetic, and geometry: harmony, system, and balance. The building blocks were all of the same material, which man calls the life essence. It was a power sent out from God, a primary ray, as man thinks of it, which by changing the length of its wave and the rate of its vibration became a pattern of differing forms, substance, and movement. This created the law of diversity which supplied endless designs for the pattern. God played on this law of diversity as a person plays on a piano, producing melodies and arranging them in a symphony.

If the building blocks are, as Cayce suggested, 'music, arithmetic, and geometry', then there is no mystery that God loves playing with numbers in our birth date and in the events of our life. Or is that a smile I see on His face?

5
Dances with Wolves

The great Indian medicine man, Black Elk, said:

> The first great peace, which is the most important, is that which comes within the souls of men when they realise their relationship, their oneness, with the universe and all its powers, and when they realise that at the centre of the universe dwells Wakan-Tanka,[30] and that this centre is really everywhere, it is within each of us. But above all you should understand that there can never be peace between nations until there is first known that fine peace which, as I have often said, is within the souls of men.[31]

Black Elk was an Oglala Sioux. He experienced a 'great vision' while standing on Harney Peak in the Black Hills of Dakota. Describing this vision he said, 'I was seeing in a sacred manner the shapes of all things in the spirit, and the shape of all things as they must live together as one being.' He understood from his vision that 'anywhere is the centre of the world'. He meant by this that we are each at the centre of the web of life. Whatever the mysterious link is between distant electrons that enables instant communication between them, it means that there is no distance between us. A way of envisioning this is through the image of the maypole, or of the sacred pole used in ritual dances. Each dancer is connected to the maypole by a ribbon. Whichever way the dancers move the pole remains at their centre, and each individual is connected with all the others through the pole and ribbons. If we take the pole to represent what is at the centre or base of all of us, a point beyond time and space, then not only do we link with all things through the centre, but we are also at the centre of things through the link. This is similar to the recent findings of astronomers that there is no centre to the universe. No matter where one stands in it, you are at the centre.

Of course, Black Elk was not the only seer to say that we each are at-one with the primal life and consciousness of the universe. The Upanishads call it 'Tat tvam asi', which means 'Thou art That'. Not only are you at the centre, but in essence you are the centre.

Fritjof Capra writes in *The Tao of Physics* about this one-in-all, and all-in-one experience. He says, 'Since we have no direct experience of the four-dimensional world of space-time, it is extremely difficult to imagine how a single particle can contain all other particles, and at the same time be part of them.'[32] But many of us do at times touch this expanded awareness. As Jacob Boehme, the German peasant mystic, wrote: 'Heaven and earth with all their inhabitants, and moreover God himself, is in man.'[33] When we see with eyes of the spirit, then we can, like William Blake, 'see a World in a Grain of Sand / And a Heaven in a Wild Flower'. We will see the animals and plants in the dance of life with us, all connected in rhythm.

Ask and it will be given

An amazing aspect of coincidences is that this mystical, or at least, subjective awareness of our connection with creation, is often expressed in terms of events rather than internal experience. Linda Clark became aware of this after attending a birthday party for the famous dolphin researcher John Lilly. Lilly's work was in the study of alien language, so he was trying to discover if humans and dolphins could communicate. This fascinated Linda, and she longed to make friends with a dolphin, even to the point of begging one of Lilly's associates to let her spend time in one of the dolphin tanks. The following day, as Linda looked out at the evening scene from her beach-front window, she was amazed to see two dolphins stranded on the shore. She immediately phoned the emergency services for help. Each service she contacted explained to her that the dolphins would certainly die. They were probably sick, and out of water they would only live for a few hours.

Not content to wait for the authorities to act, Linda went to the dolphins with pots of water to keep them cool and wet. At her first contact the dolphins, a female and calf, shuddered anxiously, but when Linda spoke to them and lay next to them, their anxiety disappeared. Through the long hours of the night Linda poured water over the dolphins and spoke to them, encouraging them not to give up. Her clothes became soaked with water so often she had to change five times. Eventually, with the dawn, a rescue crew arrived and managed to lift the dolphins back into the sea. A marine biologist later said that he was amazed the dolphins survived, and it was only the second time in a century that the species, a deep-water variety, had been stranded on a beach in Southern California.

On a TV show, Linda stressed what an amazing coincidence it was that her desire to know a dolphin was followed within hours by her experience as helper and friend of two of the wonderful animals.

In previous generations, and in most older cultures, a great deal of folklore surrounded animals in their relationship with humans. The unusual behaviour of black birds such as crows, that often feed on dead carcases, was thought to be a sign of someone's death. The American Indian peoples often recognised a special affinity between an animal and an individual. In a dream or a vision a person would receive an indication of that link. From then on they would never kill that animal, and they would look to it for guidance, not only in dreams, but in daily life.

Animals are brothers and sisters

Among African tribal peoples such links are also taken seriously. Each clan has a totem animal they must never kill, even if in general it is a food animal. This is perhaps like the sacred cows in India. Cave paintings showing animals often represent this special affinity, and also the symbolic meaning of each creature. This arose because the behaviour of each animal explained many things to human observers. Credo Mutwa, describing a cave painting from his knowledge of traditional tribal beliefs, says:

> Moving on to a second impala shown upside down with what looked like blood pouring from her mouth, he said, 'When the time came, the mother impala gave birth to her young. It was delivered into this world, but she herself died. Here you see her body. And next to it a young antelope licking its own back. They that have no parents must look

> after themselves. That is the meaning of this painting. It is the story of life and death. It is what we call Noka ya bophelo, the river of life, of continuity. It shows how life is given and life is taken, but Life goes on!'[34]

It is this symbolic and mysterious aspect of animals that is often involved in some of their synchronistic behaviour. Carl Jung noticed such events in his dealings with clients. He described one such coincidence as follows:

> For instance, I walk with a woman patient in a wood. She tells me about the first dream in her life that had made an everlasting impression upon her. She had seen a spectral fox coming down the stairs in her parental home. At this moment a real fox comes out of the trees not 40 yards away and walks quietly on the path ahead of us for several minutes. The animal behaves as if it were a partner in the human situation.

These experiences deeply impressed Jung, and led him to define a theory to explain them. He came to believe that our internal world of personal experience is not separated from the external world of events. But he did say that synchronistic events were nevertheless not causally evoked. In other words, the thoughts and actions of the individual do not cause the event in the way that striking a match and applying the flame to paper would cause the paper to burn.

One synchronistic event that most impressed Jung concerned a patient who defied all attempts at help with rigid rationalism. He describes the woman as 'intellectually inaccessible'. Through her excellent education she always felt she knew better. So Jung contented himself with hoping that something unexpected would occur that would question her rational theories. Soon after this decision he was sitting, 'listening to her flow of rhetoric', with his back to the window of the room. She described an impressive dream in which she had been given an expensive piece of jewellery in the form of a golden scarab beetle. While she was in the middle of telling this dream, Jung heard a gentle tapping on the window. He turned and saw a large insect trying to fly into the room. When he opened the window the creature flew right into the darkened space, and Jung caught it in his hand as it entered. He said:

> It was a scarabaeid beetle, or common rose-chafer (*Celonia aurata*), whose gold-green colour most nearly resembles that of a golden scarab. I handed this beetle to my patient with the words, 'Here is your scarab.' This experience punctured the desired hole in her rationalism and broke the ice of her intellectual resistance. The treatment could now be continued with satisfactory results.[35]

I am lifted up

This power to change our feeling state, or to speak to us beyond the limitations of words, is a powerful characteristic of many coincidental encounters with animals. A friend, Chris M., whom I met while teaching on the island of Skyros in Greece, told me such a story. During a period of depression, when he felt he had hit the lowest point, and even the weather was dark and dreary, Chris had crumpled on to the floor of his small room. Full of feelings of hopelessness, his attention was suddenly diverted from his despair by a tapping on the one tiny window of the room. Rising from the floor, he went to the window and saw a swallow hovering there. It remained for a few moments as he watched. Then on swift wings it was gone. The action of this small creature magically shifted Chris's mood, and he felt ready to try to meet the difficulties of his life again. As part of the change he decided to move south from Scotland to the Mediterranean, where the brightness and warmth would support his lighter mood. Having taken the train to Brindisi in Italy, he boarded the ferry to make the sea crossing to Greece. As the boat pulled away from the harbour, Chris stood at the bows looking out to sea, wondering what lay ahead. Suddenly a single swallow appeared just in front of the bow of the boat. For several minutes it kept its position, leading the ferry out to sea. Who can tell what it was doing there? But for Chris it was a confirmation of his journey toward a fuller and happier life. He was taking the right direction.

Animals, through the way they sometimes coincidentally weave their life into ours, may confirm us in other ways than personal growth or direction. Steve Nicholls's experience, quoted at the beginning of Chapter Two, is an example. Steve, in a 'dream', walked downstairs from his bedroom into the family living room. To remind you of the scene I quote again what Steve said:

> Everything in the room was as it should be, as if I was awake … I could see the clock on the mantelpiece, and the time of the 'dream' was just past 11:00 p.m. We had a dog at the time and he was lying in front of the fireplace. My father was sitting in a chair reading a book. As I focused my attention on the dog, he raised his head and started whining. He then rose and began pawing the ground. I was convinced that I was in this room and not just dreaming, as I could see very clearly what was going on.

Steve's father admitted that the dog had whined and pawed the ground at that time of night. The co-occurrence between Steve's dream and the dog's actions turns something that could be 'explained away' into an extraordinary experience. The supersenses of Steve's dog, enabling it to be aware of Steve's mobile-self, confirmed for Steve that there are sides to the human mind that are not known to present scientific theories. So apart from confirming what Steve felt about his dream – that it was an experience of reality – the dog also pushed against the boundaries of Steve's father's disbelief.

You create your environment

The last point is important in that belief, or disbelief, is a powerful force. Like a solid wall, belief/disbelief can act as a barrier against information and relationship. Allied with fear, disbelief can become a fortress against change or learning. It is a fortress against which argument is usually an ineffective weapon, as with Jung and his client. But sometimes a little old hound dog can breach the wall, or it might be a beautiful insect that is the enabler.

When I was eighteen, and stationed in Germany in the RAF, I had a similar experience to that of Steve. It also involved my dog, Vince, who was a beautiful and loving Alsatian. What happened to me didn't seem like a dream. It was even more vivid and real than waking life, although of a much different quality. I had suddenly been awoken from sleep by an intense feeling of rushing upward, and expansion. Everything was black until I could suddenly see my body asleep on the bed below me. Then, with my knees clasped to my chest – not at all the Superman image – I flew way above the ground across the summer evening landscape. At one point I could see ripples of energy rising from the ground. I wondered if this was people praying. Then the flying ended and I was immediately at home in London.

This was such an enormously impressive experience that I stood for a while stunned, trying to understand what was happening to me. My mother was seated knitting, watching television, and Vince was asleep in front of the gas fire. My father was not there. Excitedly I called to my mother, 'Mum, look what's happening to me!' She obviously didn't hear me, and this was incredibly puzzling because I was so real and solid to myself. I felt there must be some sort of barrier between us, so I shouted to her, trying to 'get through', or attract her attention. Physically she still carried on knitting. But a part of her, that felt to me as if it were 'downstairs', underneath her usual actions and awareness, responded. From that part of her there was no separation between us. At the same time Vince jerked awake, having apparently heard me shout. He looked around to where I was standing behind our settee, and came bounding to me, howling and barking as if in agony. This was something he always did if I had been away for a while and returned home. He was crazily in love with me and didn't mind showing it.

There the experience ended. I awoke back in Germany, with my body feeling as heavy as lead after having experienced the fluid lightness of life apart from it.

Later, when I checked with my mother what had happened that evening, she told me that my father, a part-time musician, had been out playing in a band, and she had been sitting alone knitting. Most importantly, Vince had suddenly reared up from sleep and rushed to the back of the settee, howling and leaping about for no reason she could see.

My dog saw my spirit

My experience was strong enough not to need Vincent's corroboration of action. But his loving response did remain a strength in face of cynical doubts that darken us all at some time. What was more important to me was his response itself. That this coincided with my own attempt to communicate was profoundly meaningful. This because my mother's response was paradoxical. She both did and didn't respond. If the dead exist in the way I did during that flight of awareness, as a bodiless personality, I can understand their frustration in trying to let the people they love know what is happening to them. Although I was totally and vividly real to myself, even to feeling completely solid, my mother, in her physically observable personality, had no awareness of me at all. But some part of herself, of which she was unconscious, responded to my call. However, Vincent heard, saw and responded.

If I had been physically present and Vince barked and howled on my return, that would not be considered a coincidence. But as my experience is thought by science to be a purely subjective one, and my mother, as a physical witness, did not see me, then the event is synchronous. For me the experience has remained a source of strength in meeting the materialism of our times. It has also been a great learning experience. For instance, was the part of my mother's mind that responded to me what psychology calls her unconscious? If so, is the unconscious similar to the sensitivity in Vince that responded so fully to me? Perhaps what was active in Vince is also alive in us humans, but often covered over by thinking and daily concerns. Maybe this heightened awareness breaking through to consciousness is what we call intuition. I believe it is, and when we listen to our intuitive ideas and feelings, we are more in tune with the great web of sentient life.

Animals appear to live to a much greater degree from this intuitive awareness than we do. This is why they interact with us synchronously in the way they do. This is obvious in the case that appeared in the *San Francisco Call-Bulletin*. Welcome Lewis travelled to San Francisco from Los Angeles with her boxer dog. As she was staying in a hotel she decided to take her dog to Lafayette Park for a walk. She found a place to leave her car alongside the park, but her dog absolutely refused to get out of the car. He was agitated and kept barking. So after a few minutes Welcome returned to the car and drove back to the hotel, where the dog got out without any fuss. The next day Welcome drove past the park, and noticed that a huge tree had come down, smashing a car exactly where she had parked on the previous day. Fascinated, she made enquiries and discovered the tree had fallen minutes after she had driven away.

Of course, the intuition of animals is proverbial, as for instance with the stories told about rats deserting a sinking ship, or animals leaving volcanoes that are about to erupt. The actor Raymond Massey and his wife had strange experiences that show a new facet of these old folktales. The Masseys had purchased a house in the East 80s of New York's Manhattan. Opposite was a mansion that was empty when they first arrived, but was later owned by a well-known woman in the town. When talking with the Masseys, the woman complained that the house was infested with mice that she couldn't get rid of. Shortly after that the Masseys were astonished to see a horde of mice leaving the house. They appeared agitated and dazed. Not long after that the woman committed suicide. The house was then purchased by a 'wealthy playboy'. During his occupancy, the Masseys once more saw the fleeing horde of desperate mice. The playboy's death followed shortly afterwards, making front-page news.

A well-known businessman was the next owner. While looking after a window-box one morning, Mrs Massey again saw the ominous mice exodus from the mansion. A few days later the businessman, while flying his private plane, crashed into the Hudson River and drowned.

Animals reflect our feelings

There is a strong suggestion, in the case of the deserting mice, that our life and the way we live it, is inextricably interwoven with everything around us. The mice certainly appear to have been influenced by the lives of the people occupying the same house. Most of the time we fail to recognise this influence that we have on others around us. We might think our influence is through what we say or do directly as an action. But what flows from us, and to us, is much subtler than that. People near to death, or during a death experience such as cardiac arrest, have their workaday personality stripped away, and live more fully in their intuitive unconscious. Then they see just how extensively their life interacts with others. During such an experience, P. H. Atwater experienced what he described as:

> A total reliving of every thought I had ever thought, every word I had ever spoken, and every deed I had ever done; plus the effect of each thought, word and deed on everyone and anyone who had ever come within my environment or sphere of influence, whether I knew them or not (including unknown passers-by on the street).[36]

Many psychic experiences appear to be the result of what is going on in the lives of those around us or close to us emotionally. Emily, who had a near-death-experience due to a road accident, said that she remembered her whole life, and was able to feel her own feelings and the feelings of everyone else she was involved with, connected with all the events in her life.

Animals are part of eternity

When looking at our coincidental link with animals, this collective awareness is important to remember. Sometimes this awareness even transcends a given lifetime. It is illustrated by one of the most astonishing coincidences that I have come across concerning an animal. Greg[37] was driving with his family and dachshund dog across an area of the US he had never previously visited. They were passing through farming country, it was fine, and the dog had its nose out of the window sampling the new smells. Suddenly the dog became agitated and leapt out of the window of the moving car. It recovered from the fall and ran headlong across a field towards a farmhouse. Greg stopped the car and immediately chased after it, wondering what was going on, as the dog had never before done such a thing. On arriving at the farmhouse he found his dog, still excited, trying to get into an outbuilding. He explained as best he could to the woman owner of the farm, Kath, why he was there, and she opened the door to the barn. The dog immediately ran to a ladder leading to a hay loft. Despite its shape, the dachshund climbed the ladder, and whining, ran around the loft sniffing and searching. Then, having searched, it became quiet and from then on was normal again.

Kath, having witnessed this, told Greg a strange story. Some years before, her son had owned a farm dog, a bitch, whom he loved. He had trained the bitch to climb the ladder in the outbuilding, because it was fun to see her running up and down. One cold winter when she had her first litter of pups, the place she chose to give birth was up in the hay loft. Perhaps she felt it was a safe place for them to be. Shortly afterwards a phone call came reporting an emergency with a family member. Kath was upset, her son was away, and she rushed out of the house, only realising later that the dog was locked in the house and couldn't get to her pups. When Kath got home three days later and opened the door, the dog streaked out of the house to the barn to feed its pups. It was so frantic that it fell from near the top of the ladder because of the ice, and died from the fall. What Kath felt that she and Greg had witnessed was the return of that mother to satisfy a frustrated need to find its pups. Even death did not end that love.

6
Crossing the Bridge

Perhaps the most impressive of all historical coincidences is that involving John Chapman. Although John was a simple peddler and tinker who lived in the fifteenth century, he was the major financial contributor to the building of Swaffham Church, in the county of Norfolk. John's riches did not come about from trading, but from an extraordinary series of coincidences recorded in the church. These are in the form of carved wooden statuettes of John and his dog on the vicar's stall. John's wife is carved opposite this stall on the north side. There are also bench ends on the front pews of the nave.

The legend of how John came to be a rich man is that after long years of trying to survive as a tinker and peddler in Swaffham market, he had a dream. In his dream he was told that if he went to London and stood on London Bridge, he would meet a man who would give him news of great riches. To travel that distance in those days was a major venture. John had no horse, and there were no coaches at that period, so he would have to walk and lodge where he could, probably in hay-stacks. Despite these difficulties, and the ridicule for believing in a dream, he walked the hundred miles. The records tell that he made it in three days.

John stayed on the bridge for two days, waiting to hear the wonderful news his dream had promised. Nobody came. There was no news. On the third day John was preparing to go home, wondering what taunts and ridicule he would meet back in Swaffham. London Bridge was actually like a normal street, even though it spanned water, with shops and houses built on it. One of the shopkeepers, having seen John standing for three days near his shop, came out and asked him what he was doing on the bridge. John told him the strange story of his dream. Without telling his name or origin, he said he had waited three days but there was still no sign of the dream being realised. The shopkeeper laughed and said:

> I am sorry for thee, my good friend. Now if I heeded dreams I might have proved myself as very a fool as thou hast; for it is not long since I dreamt that at a place called Swaffham Market, in Norfolk, dwells one John Chapman, a peddler. He hath a tree in his back garden, so I dreamed, under which is buried a pot of money. Now suppose I journeyed all the way thither because of that dream in order to dig for that money, what a fool I should be!

Returning home with more hope than when he left, John dug under his pear tree. Not far under the surface he found a pot. Pulling off the lid, he saw it was filled with gold and silver coins. But on the lid words were inscribed. So John, being uneducated, took the lid to local schoolboys who read it for him. It was a verse, and ran:

> Under me doth lye
> Another much richer than I.

John immediately returned and once more delved into the earth. There, under where he had already dug, was an even larger store of treasure. Secretly he removed and hid it. In fact his neighbours knew nothing about his wealth. Despite his treasure he lived as he had lived before. So when the church needed renovation, John was taxed the small amount his normal station required. The eighteenth-century historian Francis Blomefield comments on this:

> But he, knowing his own ability, came to the church and desired the workmen to show him their model, and to tell him what they esteemed the charge of the North-Isle would amount to; which when they told him, he presently undertook to pay them for building it, and not only that, but a very tall and beautiful tower steeple.

Together we make a whole

John Chapman's experience illustrates, either as fact, or as a metaphor, that we are each a part of a whole. Without the shopkeeper, John would not have gained his treasure. Without John's dream and endeavour, there would have been no discovery. Without all the pieces coming together there would be no memorial to John and his life in Swaffham Church of St Peter and St Paul.

Coincidences bridge the apparent gap, the felt loneliness and the separation that are a part of human existence. They create links between people, or exhibit aspects of bonding that are usually hidden or mysterious. Not only does the strange synchronicity of some events create a bridge between the living, but the dark land of danger and death is also occasionally illuminated in the same way.

Chris Graham and Steve Ashton came face to face with this mystery when they arranged to meet friends at an upstate New York park. The park had great recreational facilities, with boating and fishing, and Chris and Steve had arranged to meet their friends at exactly 1 p.m. But it was quite a drive to the park, and as they travelled the New York State Thruway, the car burst a tyre. Being young and experienced, it only took them fifteen minutes to put the spare wheel on and be on their way again. However, after a short stop at a Thruway service area, the car refused to start. The battery was flat and Steve didn't have any cables to get power from someone else's battery. It took them half an hour before they got started again. They went over the speed limit trying to make up lost time, wondering if their friends would wait. It didn't help, though. They were pulled over by the police and given a ticket.

They were now an hour late, but Steve still felt they could find their friends in whatever activity they were involved. 'It's not far now,' he said. But he had not counted on the car letting them down again. As they pulled off the Thruway the engine coughed and died. It took an hour for the garage truck to arrive, and when they reached the garage they were told it would take another two hours to fix.

Steve is an all-through optimist. 'The park is only twenty minutes away,' he said. 'Let's go see if we can find them.' They were four hours late when they entered the park. They went to the arranged place of meeting near the lake, but nobody was there. 'This is not a good day,' Chris grumbled.

Suddenly their troubles were forgotten as screams for help reached them from the lake. Two small boys were struggling in the water. 'Help us,' they were shouting. Chris and Steve were certified lifeguards. They dived into the lake and pulled out the boys, who were drowning.

When the boys were safe, Chris and Steve, trembling from the water and the emergency, looked at each other. Their agreement was mutual. If they hadn't got to the lake at exactly the time they did, the boys would have died. [38]

Is this really happening?

Researchers investigating synchronous events such as that experienced by Chris and Steve often look for an explanation in other directions than that of a sentient universe and personally creative interaction in the web of life. One such explanation is that coincidences possibly arise from positive paranoia. That is, we seek meaning in the world, and project something positive on to chance events. If you have ever experienced a coincidence linking your experience in a strange way with someone else, such explanations will not be satisfying. Perhaps the explanation I have offered of a sentient and responsive universe does not satisfy either. But in face of a powerful coincidence, we have to admit we are confronted by a mystery.

Such an event occurred to my first wife Brenda and me, and involved our daughter Helen. At the time we lived in a two-bedroom house in Amersham, Bucks, in the UK. We had three children at that time, Mark, Helen and Neal, aged between eight and four. As we only had two bedrooms the children all slept in one room. The door to this was opposite our own bedroom door at the top of a long flight of thirteen stairs. For some reason, the children had started waking at about two or three o'clock in the morning, and playing as if it were time to get up. Half asleep, Brenda would go into their room, tell them off for waking so early, get them back into bed, and return to bed herself.

On the night of the event we had slept soundly, but Brenda and I were woken by the sound of the children's door handle turning, then the sound of bumping footsteps going down the stairs. As we listened we both had the same thought – 'Oh no, it's the children awake again.' The children had never ventured downstairs before, but Brenda, thinking dark thoughts of having once more to get up in the middle of the night, went out to investigate. I heard her switch the stairs light on, go down the stairs and switch the sitting room light on. I followed her via the sounds of her movement as she looked in the kitchen and even toilet – we didn't have a bathroom. Then up she came again and opened the children's door – strange because we had assumed it had been opened. When she came back into our room she looked puzzled and a little scared. 'They're all asleep and in bed,' she said.

We talked over the mystery for some time, trying to understand just how we had heard the door handle rattle, then footsteps going down the stairs, yet the door wasn't open. Also, the door handles on our doors were too high for the children to reach without standing on a chair. There was a stool in the children's bedroom which they used for that, yet it wasn't even near the door when Brenda opened it.

Having no answer to the puzzle, we stopped talking and settled to wait for sleep again. But suddenly a noise came from the children's bedroom. It sounded like the stool being dragged and then the door handle turning again, but the door not opening. 'You go this time,' Brenda said, obviously disturbed.

I opened our door quickly just in time to see the opposite door handle turn again. Still the door didn't open. I reached across, turned the handle and slowly opened the door. It stopped as though something was blocking it. Just then Helen's small face peered around the door – high because she was standing on the stool. Puzzled by what had happened, I was careful what I said to her. 'What do you want?' I asked.

Unperturbed, she replied, 'I want to go to the toilet.' The toilet was downstairs, through the sitting room and through the kitchen.

Now I had a clue, so I asked, 'Did you go downstairs before?'

'Yes,' she said, 'but mummy sent me back to bed!'

The inexplicable might show us what really is real

I had certainly heard the descending footsteps, but I had also heard Brenda open the door to the children's bedroom, along with her own witness, so I knew Helen had not physically descended the stairs. Nevertheless, two of us had heard the opening door and the footsteps. Helen also claimed she had been down, but Brenda had sent her back. So there was synchronicity between three people's experience, but no physical evidence of the descent. Therefore, had Helen dreamt the incident? If so, how did we hear the door handle turning and the footsteps descending? Was this positive paranoia? I don't think so. Nor do I think it was a non-causal event, or chance collection of incidents. What I do believe is that our present psychological theories of consciousness and mind are inadequate to explain such events.

My own best explanation is that consciousness is not something that is separated and individual. Through our body senses and language we define an area of our own personal experience that we call self. Through the perspective of this 'self' we are aware of having a distinct personality with unique experiences and memory. This personal self is rather like a highlighted area within a three-dimensional, or multi-dimensional, field. This is what I have previously called the ocean of sentience, or ocean of mind. Our personal awareness colours the water with individual memories and experience. Our body brain helps us to tune into what is individually ours within the ocean of sentience, just as a radio tunes into particular signals within the huge range of radio waves acting on its aerial. However, if we explore the depths of our personal awareness, delve into what we call the unconscious, we find that our personal self begins to shade into a universal consciousness. The waters of self and the waters of the ocean are not separated. This universal consciousness is what Jung called the collective unconscious. Other cultures have given it other names – the ocean of Brahm, for instance, in Hinduism. Within Buddhism there is also the phrase, 'the dewdrop slips into the shining sea'. This illustrates the individual becoming aware of melting the boundaries of his or her personal awareness, and becoming aware of the ocean of sentience within which they exist.

Returning to the experience with Helen, the analogy of the ocean is a helpful one for several reasons. If Helen's mind was limited to the boundaries of her body, then her dream, if that's what it was, of going to the toilet, would have remained merely a personal fantasy. However, if her body is immersed in an ocean of consciousness – perhaps the fundamental principle of life – of which her personal awareness is an unseparated part, then there is the possibility of her mind being active anywhere in that ocean. After all, the foundation of her existence is the ocean. In this scheme, mind is everywhere at once, but is usually limited in its perceptions by the input of the body senses, and by the concepts of mind arising from the language and cultural viewpoint.

I am with you – now and always

Glimpses that we do gain of the greater extension of consciousness, and our unbroken link with other people, are usually translated by the brain, and by our constant activity to create meaning. Such meaning is expressed as imagery and experience consistent with the impressions we gain through our senses. Understanding how dreams work helps in gaining a clearer insight into this. While we dream, even abstract feelings or concepts such as love or justice are translated into the imagery of people, objects and places, and felt to be real events in which we take part. As an example, suppose we mentally made contact with a being who does not have a physical form, but exists as an energy field. We would still tend to 'see' this being as somebody exterior to us, having some sort of shape and dimension in space and time. This is classically illustrated in the imagery of religion. Studying the basics of most world religions, human consciousness, even the body, are not seen as distinctly separate from the divine. Nevertheless we still talk of the divine – God – as having separate existence, as being something apart from ourselves, and maybe even having a gender. Tragically, many of us still see the cultural and social differences given to the abstract divine as meaning that Allah is different to God, and Brahm is different to Jehovah. Fortunately, however, most of the world's great explorers of consciousness have moved beyond this dualism. Ramakrishna describes his own first experience of this as follows:

> The last barrier fell and my spirit immediately precipitated itself beyond the plane of the 'conditional', and I lost myself in Samadhi (unconditioned bliss). The Universe was extin-

> guished. Space itself was no more. At first the shadows of ideas floated in the obscure depths of the mind. Monotonously a feeble consciousness of the ego went on ticking. Then that stopped too. Nothing remained but Existence. The soul was lost in Self. Dualism was blotted out. Finite and infinite space were as one.

There are many different ways of explaining this same paradox of experiencing oneself as an individual, yet realising oneself as an unseparated part of the whole. Edgar Cayce, using the word soul to refer to individual experience, and God to represent the whole, says:

> When a soul returns to God it becomes aware of itself not only as part of God, but as part of every other soul, and everything. What is lost is the ego – the desire to do other than the will of God. When the soul returns to God the ego is voluntarily relinquished; this is the symbology of the crucifixion.

Sai Baba of Shirdi had a subtle way of describing this human situation. Talking with his student Nana, Baba had pointed out that some of the greatest teachings showed that human existence and the divine were one and the same. As the divine, each of us has infinite knowledge, as mentioned in a previous chapter. Our usual experience, though, is of comparative ignorance, and so in seeking to realise our divine nature we seek instruction or knowledge. Sai Baba commented on this situation by saying to Nana:

> The disciple is a being whose essential nature is Knowledge. Therefore there is no need to give him knowledge but simply to remove the veil of ignorance that hides the existent Knowledge. This, of course, is not to be done at one stroke, since the disciple is immersed in age-old ignorance and needs repeated instruction, perhaps through life after life. And what is this instruction through speech about what is beyond speech? Isn't it like removing the cover? Ignorance conceals the pre-existent Knowledge just as

water plants cover the surface of a pond. Clear away the plants and you have the water. You don't have to create it; it is already there.

Looking beyond what the eyes see

We all live in the midst of this amazing mystery that is life. Sometimes we glimpse beyond the surface of this mystery into greater dimensions, as Brenda and I did that night with Helen. The glimpses we gain, given form and cultural context by our interpretative brain, nevertheless give us wonderful insights into the less physical places of life. They show us that life is a continuum, and love links us with others we may have thought were dead and gone.

A couple were worried about their young daughter, Carol,[39] witnessing the deterioration of her grandmother, who was in her eighties and dying from the effects of heart disease, arthritis and old age. As the grandmother was being cared for in the home, it was easy for Carol to enter the bedroom to be with her grandmother. But the parents discouraged their daughter from spending too much time with her grandmother, as they thought it was a distressing sight for a nine-year-old. Nevertheless, finding herself drawn to be with her grandmother, Carol went to her one day, but returned to her parents within a few minutes with a puzzled expression. 'Mommy,' she said, 'There are two grandmothers. I saw two grannies in the room. First I talked to granny and then a lighted lady named Beth came and talked to me and granny. Then they left together.'

When the mother went with Carol into the grandmother's room, they discovered that she had died. Carol's simple and clear description of what she had seen changed her mother's view of death. Especially so as Carol did not know that her great grandmother's name was Beth.[40]

The coincidental aspects of Carol's vision were that Beth was the name of her great grandmother, and that Carol saw what she did at the moment of her grandmother's death.

Critics of this might say that Carol had most likely heard the name Beth at some time, and that she hallucinated the vision of her two grandmothers leaving the room. The argument about having heard the name Beth is an insoluble one. Any critic can argue that a person's memories are false, and there is no answer that will convince the critic otherwise. But the question of hallucinations in connection with such experiences, or even with drugs, is no longer permissible. The suggestion is that we are prone to create almost any imagery we like, and that drugs create imagery completely unrelated to the psyche of the person. Years of research into unconscious functioning and imagery show that every fantasy is linked very directly to the psyche of the person, and that drugs do not bend this rule. Anybody who has explored the unconscious deeply will have personal experience of this.[41]

Kastenbaum, in exploring the viewpoint of critics, mentions the occurrence of negative and even terrifying imagery in connection with some near-death experiences, as a possible indication of them being simply the brain's method of fantasy in a high-stress situation. In this theory the NDE is seen as a way of removing one's awareness from a stress event. The critical question asked is that if the NDE experience is a real perception of a world existing after death, then why do some people see this world full of demonic figures and as terrifying?

Dreams are more than dreams

Sometimes such questions seem naïve, especially when asked by said professors and doctors. I mean by this that it is common experience in everyday life that we observe a wide variety of responses to the world. Some people suffer high anxiety about even such a common experience as riding in, or driving, a car. For others the experience is pleasurable or stimulating. If we were to put these differences in response into imagery, the first would be hellish, and the other heavenly. Also, in any subjective experience, such as an NDE, or when the threshold between conscious and unconscious weakens, one meets imagery related to trauma that has not been dealt with. Stanislav Grof's description of people meeting birth trauma is convincingly that of hell and demons.[42] Meeting a near-death-experience is no different. Any traumas or fears you had not dealt with in life would be met as the threshold broke down. These fears and traumas would be presented, just as dreams present them, as real external environment and events. In ancient occult teachings of the Western tradition, this was called meeting the Guardian of the Threshold. The guardian required you to meet the negative aspects of your past experience and actions before you could reach the positive wider life. Isn't this exactly what people describe when they give details of a full life review as they are dying?

Fortunately, many so called 'hallucinations' provide synchronistic information, and so cannot be discarded as simply fantasies aiding the person to disassociate themselves from pain and fear, or as a stress response. One of the most powerful of these is described in *Closer to the Light* by Dr Morse. It was told to him by a physician who had witnessed the case.

A pregnant woman, Andrea, experienced difficulties during the delivery of her baby.[43] The placenta was separating prematurely, and the baby's head was at an angle to make its delivery extremely difficult. When the child was eventually born it was discovered that he had a severe brain haemorrhage. His condition was so bad he had to remain in the intensive care unit of the small hospital. Andrea did not want him moved to a larger hospital as she wished to be near him at all times. The doctors caring for him did not press her to make the move as he was so ill, and no treatment was possible. Besides the brain damage, the baby boy had severe cerebral palsy and seizures. An EEG showed the abnormality. Dr Morse says, 'These are afflictions from which children simply don't recover. If they survive infancy, they spend their lives severely retarded.' Andrea was told the diagnosis but she stayed with her baby nearly 24 hours a day for months.

While Andrea was with her child late one night, she looked up and saw a 'being of light' enter the room. She described the being as having the same form as a human, but not decidedly male or female. It glowed with a pale light as it spoke to her. 'Your son will be all right,' it said, assuring her that her son would be normal. As the glowing being spoke to her, Andrea felt as though love poured into her body in a marvellous way. It so deeply impressed her that the next morning she told the attending medical team what had happened, and persuaded them to do another EEG to see if any change had actually occurred. When the brain-wave test was completed, it showed that Andrea's deeply sick child was completely normal, having made a full recovery.[44]

Fantasy might be an image of the real

For some people, mention of beings of light probably evokes thoughts that some people have of embellishing life with fairy lights and Easter bunnies. Fortunately the fact of Andrea's son's complete recovery shows that a process of enormous change was at work, and not just wishful thinking. The real process of change that Andrea confronted late that night might have been depicted in quite a different way if she had been born in a different culture. As a Hindu she might have seen it depicted as one of the many gods, such as Shiva. As mentioned above, our process of creating meaning out of impressions received through our senses, or from our unconscious, is one that forms apparently real people and environments that seem to be exterior to us. If we get lost in whether there is actually a being of light who has blonde hair and blue eyes, we may completely miss the point. That point is that Andrea sensed a great change acting upon her son, and felt the power of that change. Her unconscious process of image formation pictured this as a being of light. Her experience, and the message she received, coincided with actual change in her son. That change, Andrea connected with the power of love.

I am not in any way trying to suggest there are not wonderful intelligences – beings – of a different order to our experience of life in the physical body. My comments are simply to show that if our critical mind prevents us from opening to the power of coincidence that links us with loving change because of the words 'beings of light', then there are other ways of looking at the experience: ways, hopefully, that will let even the most rational among us open to the mystery of life, however it might be explained.

Coincidences link us with that mystery and with the power that might somehow enter our life from that mystery. If people in the past, and today, kneel before that mystery, then perhaps their attitude arises from a sense of its wonder. If so, then I share that wonder and awe, and feel love when confronted by it, just as Andrea did. If there are beings, intelligences, who share that love, then I reach out to them in co-operation and sympathy.

When a synchronistic event such as Andrea's occurs, we must remember that very often only certain people or animals can see the disembodied beings. When my disembodied awareness visited my mother in London, as my body slept in Germany, my mother was not aware of my presence. It was my dog who witnessed my visit. This is in no way different to our everyday experience, and is quite understandable by anyone. When we stand before a friend and think certain thoughts, the friend, even a lover, is usually totally unaware of what we are thinking except if our expression gives us away, or if we tell them. In other words, our thoughts and feelings, despite being of extreme reality to us, are usually not discernible by anyone else, except through the physical senses. If, therefore, we think of the dead, or beings of light, or of an out-of-body personality, as a focus of thoughts and feelings in the ocean of sentience, then it is understandable why we cannot see them. That is, we cannot see them with our eyes or hear them with our ordinary ears. But this is no different from not being able to know the thoughts of the living. The dead have the same difficulty communicating with us, because they are beings of thought and feeling without a body. But if we listen to our intuition and unconscious impressions, we can 'hear' them.

There are more things in heaven and earth …

Time has been taken to explain this because I believe that if we are ill at ease with such things, we shut them out of our realm of possibility. That is a great diminishment of our opportunities. Who knows when we might need extraordinary healing, or wisdom, or help? It is akin to not using the telephone to contact a friend or calling a taxi when we need to get somewhere quickly. As human beings we have the most amazing potential, as can be witnessed by some of the cases mentioned throughout these pages. We need not think of this potential in any particular form; but of course we might be predisposed to think of it in ways such as beings of light, dead relatives, pure energy, the unconscious mind, or applied creativity. Your explanation only really matters to yourself. It does not alter the fact of the potential. But your explanation may either enhance your ability to reach out for more of the possibilities of your life, or it may be a means of shutting yourself off from them.

From the viewpoint of potential and energy, as well as disembodied intelligences, this next example of coincidence is interesting.

A man, Franklin, was lying ill in a hospital room.[45] He was not taking any drugs to sedate his pain, so what happened was not drug-induced. Franklin was a religious man, believed in life after death, and probably knew that he was dying. In fact he asked the nurse and others in the room to pray for him. There was a staircase in the room leading up to a second floor, and a drinking glass had been left on one of the steps. Suddenly Franklin looked at the stairs and cried out happily, 'See, the angels are coming down the stairs. The glass has fallen and broken.' Everyone in the room turned to the stairs where Franklin indicated. As they looked they saw the glass shatter in many pieces. It didn't fall, but seemed to explode. But nobody else saw any angels. Almost immediately Franklin died with a happy and serene expression on his face. The expression remained long after his death.

The coincidental link between what Franklin said and the shattering of the glass is not unusual. Perhaps we call it a coincidence, or synchronistic, simply because we cannot define what the processes are that underlie it. Therefore it may seem strange, unusual, or even disturbing. Nevertheless, such events remind us that the factors of existence that lie outside of our understanding are often potently at work in a person's life. They also point out that a coincidence is not limited to unplanned meetings, finding long-lost objects, or events. They also occur in relationships between the living and the dead.

During the great period of psychic research, at the end of the nineteenth and the beginning of the twentieth century, thousands of such unusual 'coincidences' were recorded or researched. Despite extraordinary results in this area, our general culture still remains sceptical of human potential and relationship with the transcendent reality inherent in life. Talking about this scepticism, Robert Kastenbaum, author of many books about the social and personal aspects of death and dying, asks an intriguing question.[46] It relates to the present scientific attitudes towards proof of a phenomenon. Most of today's research is done in the form of statistical analysis. So Kastenbaum asks: Is one good example enough?

He gives the example of walking along the river Thames two centuries ago. A commotion attracts your attention and you discover that a man has been pulled out of the Thames, drowned, and according to the information accepted at the time, dead. He is not breathing, and there is no heartbeat. But because you are the member of a new society that trains you to be prepared for just such a situation, you use what will later become known as artificial respiration. To the amazement, and perhaps horror or terror, of the onlookers, you bring the man back to life. He sits up and speaks.

If, in later weeks, other such bodies are pulled from the Thames, and after using the same technique they are not brought back to life, what are we to assume? Does it mean that a drowned person cannot be brought back to life? Was the one case of resuscitation meaningless? Is one good example enough?

Kastenbaum gives another example. A group of 50 people gather to test the reality of levitation. All energetically try to lift off the ground, jumping and flapping, puffing and blowing, and all fail except for uncle Charlie, who floats free and easy near the ceiling. Does this mean that levitation is impossible, because if it were not, many more people would be able to do it? Or is one good example enough?

COINCIDENCE OR WHAT?

At the end of 1907, Frederic Thompson feared for his sanity. Eighteen months previously, Thompson, a goldsmith, was compulsively urged to sketch and paint. He said the subjects he painted were not even his own choice. He told Professor James H. Hyslop, head of the American Society for Psychical Research, that Robert Swain Gifford, a dead landscape artist, was dominating him. Thompson had briefly met Gifford, but had never seen any of his work. Thompson went to an exhibition of Gifford's work in New York, only to discover that the artist had died just before his own compulsions started. While at the gallery, to his distress, Thompson heard a voice say to him, 'You see what I have done. Can you not take up and finish my work?' After that Thompson would often lose consciousness, waking to find he had completed a painting. Although Thompson's artistic gifts fell short of Gifford's, his skill increased over the months. He actually sold several paintings, and people remarked on their similarity to Gifford's work.

Because I don't understand this, does that mean it doesn't exist? What usually happens, as might have happened in the early cases of resuscitation, is that where there is no understanding of what is involved, trickery or the paranormal is suspected. So, are the synchronistic events that surround unusual personal links with the living and dead no more than trickery? Are they to do with the paranormal? Or is it that we simply do not yet know how they work? Perhaps the words coincidence and synchronistic are cover-ups for lack of knowledge.

Some of the most spectacular coincidental events in the area of links between living and dead surrounded the investigations of Mrs Leonora Piper of Boston, USA. William James, the great Harvard professor and psychologist, discovered the talents of Mrs Piper, and encouraged her to demonstrate them to other investigators. One of these was Richard Hodgson, described as a sceptical and critical lawyer. Hodgson had spent time exposing the trickery and fraud of several well-known psychics of the period. One of his most public cases was his exposure of Madame Blavatsky, at the time the central figure of the Theosophical Society. Dr Hodgson was also the research officer for the American Society for Psychical Research. Therefore when William James asked Hodgson to carry on the investigation James had started, Hodgson approached the project with the zeal of someone who was certain Mrs Piper was a fraud.

Mrs Piper was what used to be called a medium, a person who relays messages from the dead to the living, and from the living to the dead. So when Hodgson presented himself to her, she calmly told him many facts about himself, his family back in Australia, even information about dead relatives. All the information was correct. Trying another tack, Hodgson sent several anonymous people to Mrs Piper, none of whom she had ever met before, to see how she would respond. She gave them definite names of deceased relatives, along with facts and events from their lives. Astonished, Hodgson hired detectives to watch Mrs Piper to see from where she got her information. After careful surveillance they reported that she had not been in touch with anyone. But Hodgson did not give up. While he was trying other approaches, a personality spoke via Mrs Piper claiming to be George Pellew, a writer Hodgson had known prior to Pellew's death aged 32. And this is where some of the most astonishing 'coincidences' occurred.

Firstly, Pellew, speaking through Mrs Piper, gave an enormous amount of specific information about his own previous life, and about his relationship with Hodgson. The disembodied Pellew even identified 30 people he had known during his life. They were told dates of events, and names of people they knew in common. Over a hundred people Pellew had not known during his life were introduced to the disembodied Pellew as if they were people he had met. Every one was rejected. Only those who were positively known were accepted as real contacts. This consistent demonstration of an actual personality, with its own unique memories, won Hodgson over to accepting the reality of survival after physical death.

Speaking with the dead

If Mrs Piper had been throwing dice, instead of speaking from wherever in herself she gained the information, this would be like throwing double six 130 consecutive times. That is a coincidence beyond even the spectacular.

For many people, it doesn't take the wonderful talent of a Leonora Piper to assure them their friends and family survive death. A sense of connection assures them, and coincidental events inform them, of communication with departed loved ones. Sometimes this happens in a chilling way, and sometimes in a heart-warming manner. Alex Tanous, for instance, in his book *Beyond Coincidence*, tells how his psychic impressions led to a bizarre coincidence of the chilling variety. While visiting his niece at a girls' school in Leysin, Switzerland, Tanous was told that the school building had once been used as a hospital. The fourth floor of the building was now kept empty, and the girls said it was supposed to be haunted. Deciding to explore this, Tanous went to the fourth floor and opened to his intuitive impressions. He felt a chill descend on him as he began to relive what he felt were events from the past. He saw a very wealthy old woman being dragged, struggling, to the balcony, and thrown off. The murderer was a member of her own family who wanted the woman dead to inherit the great wealth. As the killing was made to look like a suicide, the murderer was never arrested.

Tanous explained his impressions to the girls at the school, and also to a group of American teachers to whom he later lectured at a college in Leysin. A member of the audience told Tanous that the author A. E. Ellis had written about just such a situation in his book *The Rack*. Tanous did not think there was anything to explore regarding this coincidence. But some time later, after a press interview in which he mentioned his own impressions and the book, someone sent him a copy of *The Rack*. Only then did Tanous see that Ellis had exactly described the incident Tanous had relived, including the opinion that it had been wrongly called suicide. Yet stranger, the story was set in Switzerland and the hospital was at Leysin. Lastly, *The Rack* is non-fiction! It seems that the murdered woman wanted her story known.

A more heart-warming incident involves the great Italian writer Dante. Boccaccio, a contemporary of Dante, and the author of his biography, tells how Dante's great work, *Paradiso*, appeared unfinished at his death. The last thirteen cantos of the work could not be found despite searching for several months. Friends and disciples of Dante eventually induced two of his sons, Jacopo and Piero, to complete the work themselves that it might be published. But before attempting this, Jacopo had an impressive dream. In it his father came to him, 'clothed in the purest white, and his face resplendent with an extraordinary light; and he, Jacopo, asked him if he lived, and Dante had replied: "Yes, but in

My nephew went on holiday to Minehead. While he was there his grandmother died. But to avoid spoiling his holiday we didn't tell him of her death. While he was away, his mother received what appeared to be a message from him on her telephone answering machine. Strangely, it did not seem to be his voice, but the message was, 'I don't know how I'm going to live without her. I am missing her already.' This deeply upset his mother, and when she investigated how it had come about, she discovered he had purchased a new mobile phone. While playing with it he had dialled her number, and the message was a voice on the TV or radio.

the true life, not our life."' Then Jacopo asked him if he had completed his work, and if so, where were the missing cantos. 'To this Dante seemed to answer: "Yes, I finished it", and then took him, Jacopo, by the hand and led him into that chamber in which he, Dante, had been accustomed to sleep when he lived in this life. Touching one of the walls, he said: "What you have sought for so much is here"; and at these words both Dante and sleep fled from Jacopo at once.'

Although it was late into the night, Jacopo went to the home of his father's friend and disciple, Pier Giardino, and together they set off to the house Dante had lived in prior to his death. They woke the present owner and after explaining their mission, were led to the bedchamber in which Dante had slept. There, behind a mat hanging on the wall, a small window was discovered. In this window space were the cantos, now moulding after eight months in the damp place. In this way the *Divine Comedy* was completed.

Although certain reported communications between the living and dead appear trivial, when a powerful dream coincides with reality, as Jacopo's dream did, they often include important information. Mr Batchelder was a Harvard graduate, whose grandfather had made a will that Batchelder had the courage to tell him was unfair to the family. The old man was well known for his stubbornness and hard-headedness, so Batchelder thought his comments would go unheeded. Eventually the grandfather died, and the will that was thought unfair was read and put in the hands of the executors. Soon afterwards, however, Batchelder heard the old man's voice during the night. With firm emphasis he said, 'You were right about that first will. I made another. Don't rest till you find it!'

The voice was so loud it woke Batchelder, and as soon as was practical he went to his grandfather's house and started searching. There were drawers full of notes, manuscripts – he was a writer and editor of a magazine – bills and piles of letters. Eventually, after a long search, he found the new will among a heap of other papers. It was more recent than the one being executed, and had been drawn up by a lawyer other than the usual family attorney. It was completely legal, and corrected the alleged unfairness. Until he heard the strong voice of his grandfather, Batchelder maintains that he had never thought of looking for another will. That the given message turned out to be factual seemed to Batchelder like a positive communication from his surviving grandfather.

Such positive communications enter our life like rays of hope. Don Bradley gave a title to his book that has a strong message about such coincidences. It is called *Angels in a Harsh World*. Even if we are inclined to believe in the present Western view of life, in which high stress and pressure are part of the system, it may be difficult to accept the sort of interventions mentioned above. Despite the extraordinary coincidences that occur daily to people around the world, giving evidence of life's interconnectedness, and the continuance of life after death, virtually all official statements, news reports and political pronouncements proceed from a stance of intellectual cynicism. They speak as if none of the thousands of hours of research and uncountable number of human experiences ever happened. Robert Kastenbaum skilfully sums up this attitude when he writes:

> Belief in survival is the case in point. What is this belief but a mental toy? A plaything that magically granted every wish when in our youthful ambition we were greedy for all sweets and too headstrong to acknowledge limits? The vision of the 'happy ever after' was all pleasure and comfort rolled into one vast security blanket – our invincible sword to cut down all adversity and disappointments ... this belief – in survival – had its day in the childhood of the human race, a mental and cultural device intended to soften the actual experience of pain, loss and danger.

Do we need science to assure us we are alive?

As he goes on to say later, our present scientific theories, in looking at this criticism, have no way of explaining the facts of human experience, or of some aspects of research. Unfortunately, when prevailing theory cannot explain facts, facts are swept aside. Facts of experience are then explained as childish or wish-fulfilling theories. But do we need a scientific theory to assure us of what our heart tells us? Do we need proof of what we feel when we come alive, or experience a sense of wonder at the sight of a child or nature? Do we need someone else to make us confident of what brings tears of joy to our eyes?

Whether fact or theory, the following wonderful incident is a fitting end to this chapter on coincidence as a link between people, living or dead.

When my son Léon was about seven, he went from the UK to the United States with his mother and sister, to visit an aunt living there. While there his grandfather died suddenly without warning. I did not pass the news of this on to my wife because I thought she would feel it necessary to cut her visit short. On the day his grandfather died, Léon, for what appeared to his mother to be no good reason, became suddenly depressed and cried for hours. His unhappiness, he said, was because everything was dying, even the sun.

During 1986, David Young and his family attacked an elementary school in Cokeville, Wyoming. They carried a mass of weapons and explosives into the school and held 156 children hostage, threatening to kill them. Later, Young exploded the bomb, thereby destroying the whole school. Yet none of the children were hurt. Many of the youngsters were later able to describe how this miracle of escape happened. They said people who were shining with a light from within them told them how to escape safely from the school. One of the young girls explained in detail what happened. [47]

> They [the shining people] were standing there above us. There was a mother and a father and a lady holding a tiny baby and a little girl with long hair. There was a family of people. The woman told us that a bomb was going off soon and to listen to our brother. She said to be sure we did what he told us. They were dressed in white, *bright like light bulbs, but brighter around the face.* The woman made me feel good. I knew she loved me.

The girl's brother described it slightly differently:

> I didn't see anything. I just heard a voice tell me to find my little sisters and take them over by the window, and keep them there. They were playing with their friends, and they

> did not want to move. I took them to the window and helped them through.

And lastly, a six-year-old said, 'A lady told me that a bomb was going to go off soon. She said to go over by the window and hurry out.'

Sometimes it takes an extraordinary crisis to part the clouds that hide the wonder in which we live. At other times all it needs is a humble heart, or a quietness that comes from realising the futility of our own thoughts in their attempt to understand life.

7
Making the Connection

When my daughter Helen started reading Louise Hay's book, *You Can Heal Your Life*, she was particularly struck by the section on money.[48] An exercise in the book suggested looking at oneself in a mirror, saying one's name, and exclaiming, 'I love you'. While doing the exercise and asking the questions Louise suggests, Helen realised she had the feeling that she didn't deserve money. There was a strong sense that other people might deserve it but she didn't. In addressing this attitude, Helen felt she could now accept money coming to her. She entered a competition in the local newspaper – *North Devon Journal* – sure she would win. Within the week she had a letter telling her she was the winner of the competition, and enclosed was a cheque for £500.

Several times since then, Helen has had similar coincidences. She told me that each time they happen she has the feeling of certainty about the result.

One of Louise Hay's first principles is that we are each responsible for all that happens to us – 100 per cent. She believes the way we think, feel and act creates our life and the events in it. This is very different to Carl Jung's statement that coincidences are non-causal – that we have no place in creating them. Yet at the same time Jung states we are all a part of the cosmic life. Perhaps it is better to say that Jung considers our conscious intentions are not necessarily acted upon by our self, our larger, more cosmic life. This is reminiscent of the old adage, 'Man proposes, God disposes.' Perhaps a working approach to these opposites is to find a way through the middle.

When I asked for the work I wanted, as explained earlier, and the next day was offered by the *Daily Mail* exactly what I had asked for, it wasn't that I was thinking positively and felt confident of my own value. I felt awful at the time, and had a very low opinion of my worth, based on the lack of satisfying employment. So I do not concur with Louise Hay that we create out of our thinking and feeling; at least, not entirely. What I did do at that time was to ask out of my desperation. So If I learn anything when I witness what Helen did, what happened to myself, and what I learn from other people's life experiences, it is that different things work at different times. If I am to relate it to another adage, it is 'If God doesn't give us what we want, he gives us what we need.' This is especially relevant if we balance it with 'Ask, and it shall be given you.'

Overall I do believe, with Louise Hay, that out of our longing and love, out of our fear and pain, from our fantasy and work, our life emerges. But life is so full of wonders and possibilities that perhaps, deserve it or not, someone else's love showers us with blessings. Like the sunshine, we can all stand in the self-existent light of life and be warmed. Or equally, because there is room for free will, we can fall in a pit, or lock ourselves in a pig-sty for years, until we ask for help to get out. At those times it is very difficult to feel positively self-loving or self-actualising. We need help from someone else. We need to ask. With a broken leg we may need crutches for a while. With a broken heart or soul, we may need the love of another human being.

I give myself to you

Remember that life is continually dying for you. The sun pours out its energy, selflessly bringing life to earth. The living plants and creatures constantly feed you with their bodies. As in the Christian sacrament, you partake of the body of life each time you eat or drink. There is no fee asked for this. It is given. So when you seek help do not restrict your asking because you feel it will have to be paid for.

No matter what understanding you have of life and its processes, remember that it remains a mystery. As such it is beyond the struggles of your intellect to comprehend or encompass. Let this kindle some humility, and from this find a quiet mind enabling you to know directly your at-one-ment with the mystery. No great effort is required to give you that at-one-ment – neither being good or thinking positively, nor striving in meditation or prayer. The light of spirit in us is self-existent. It is not developed by us, created or earned. A Zen poem says:

Sitting quietly, doing nothing,
Spring comes, and the grass grows by itself. [49]

Jung quotes Eckhart in describing this approach to the mystery, when he says:

> The key is this: we must be able to let things happen in the psyche. For us, this becomes a real art of which few people know anything. Consciousness is forever interfering, helping, correcting, and negating, and never leaving the simple growth of the psychic processes in peace. It would be a simple enough thing to do if only simplicity were not the most difficult of all things.

The Chinese book of meditation, *The Secret of the Golden Flower*, describes this mysterious kernel of meditation as to 'do nothing but let things happen – action in non-action'.

The mystery we find in such non-effort is certainly the fount of synchronicity, and of all the other gifts arising from the fount that is life.

I had a dream that has stayed with me through the years which gave me an experience of this mystery as it enters our life. In the dream I was with several other people searching the rubble of what had been a great church. The building, ruined by some disaster such as an earthquake, or perhaps internal weakness, was now no more than a ruin of stones. Amid the rubble we searched for anything that might be salvaged. Suddenly, among the stones that at one time made up a wall near the door, I found a most wonderful chalice. Its wonder sprang not from any precious metal it was made of, nor from artistry. It was because the stemmed cup shone with its own light, a light that never diminished. Just seeing it, being near it, produced an experience of awe and marvel.

As we took up the cup we understood that it was the emanation of the light around which the church had been built. Yet out of some fear, the chalice had been hidden in the wall of the church, and stranger yet, completely forgotten. With feelings moved by this tragedy, we realised that for perhaps hundreds of years people had continued to attend the church, performing empty rituals, singing hymns, going through all the motions of worship without any direct relationship to the wonderful manifestation of the divine provided by the cup. But now we could once more place the chalice in a place where anyone could stand in its light. For it shone on all without exception, and each of us, as we were permeated by that divine light, were transformed in some way by it.

The light is an excellent symbol of what I have called the ocean of sentience. Although water is useful to depict how we can all be made of the same substance, how we merge into oneness with the ocean, or emerge as an individual person, the light has more of a sense of radiant power. It is a power that can reach across space and influence, transforming darkness. Whatever symbol we use, we need something to depict the reality of the mystery that coincidences portray to us. It is a reality that is difficult for our intellect to understand, yet is at the core of each of us equally – perhaps at the core of each particle of our being. Not only does it pervade all, but it does so in a way that is beyond time and space. Linking each of us timelessly, it enables us to connect with one another and the world in ways that normal distance and sequential time do not allow.

I touch you across infinite space

Another analogy that may illustrate this is to think of your body. Look on your two hands, or any two parts that can touch each other, as individuals, separated by space and by time. But pervading every part of your body, with its billions of cells, and countless different parts, is your sense of self. That you are aware as a person amid these countless tiny lives is a strange miracle. Remember that the atoms of any part of your body are as far apart, considering their size, as are the planets and stars of our galaxy and solar system. So, throughout that immense space and distance, your mysterious consciousness of self links all. Now, if you slowly bring two fingers of opposite hands together, you have created a coincidental meeting of widely separated individuals – of hugely separated individuals. If we can conceive of a consciousness that pervades and links all our separate personalities, then apparently unconnected coincidences are not so mysterious. It is this pervading consciousness that is suggested by the term 'ocean of sentience'.

Because it is an intimate part of us, we each have the potential to become aware of this pervading ocean of awareness, or permeating light. For instance, a feature of many near-death experiences is that the person feels drawn towards an intense yet gentle light. An NOP survey in the United States showed that over a million of the people interviewed had an experience of this light. This means they had in some way experienced an awareness of the ocean of sentience, of cosmic awareness. Peter Thompson says of this light, 'Although it was brilliant, it wasn't dazzling. I felt I was being drawn into it and the feeling was ... well the only way I can describe it is pure bliss and love.'

> Cynthia, who loves American jelly beans, especially the cinnamon-flavoured ones, visited Wells Cathedral one Saturday with her husband. She was hoping they would have time to visit a shop in Wells High Street because they sold jelly beans. However, there was no time. But as she sat in the car, Cynthia thought that if she were on a desert island, she would take American jelly beans. When they arrived home there was a little bag of jelly beans left by friends who had visited while they were away. A note read, 'We visited Wells Cathedral the other day and brought these jelly beans back.'

How can I open to the light?

To feel oneself a part of everything once again is usually as wonderful as Peter describes it. Only occasionally does it appear frightening, perhaps because we feel we are in some manner slipping away from our physical life. But the experience of merging with the ocean of life holds many possibilities. Maurice James describes his meeting thus:

> I was seeing my life flash before me, recalling my family, friends, the man on the bus, the lady in the shop — and feeling confused but happy. At this time I was in a tunnel-like black space. Just beyond a light was glowing invitingly. I was encouraged by a strong feeling to enter the light. I approached without haste as I felt the light was part of the jigsaw to which I rightfully belonged. I was peaceful, totally

> content, and I understood why I was born on earth and knew the answer to every mystery – I was not told, I just knew, the light held all the answers.[50]

For most of us, touching the light is not such an enormous experience. It comes more gently, perhaps as intuition, or as a dream. We might touch the light through an experience of healing, or of powerful psychological change or insight. Whatever way it comes, it carries with it the power and mystery we find in synchronous experience. It does this because it is the power that links us all. By spending time each day remembering our connection, we draw closer to linking with others in that light, whether in bodily life or outside it.

Although relaxation is not generally classed as a form of meditation, it is in fact one of the most potent ways of opening to the light, and of being bathed in the ocean. The light in us is self-existent. It doesn't need our effort to create it. The less we do, the more we become aware of it shining, like the wonderful light of the chalice. Throughout the ages the greatest secrets of sacred experience are expressed in such words as 'Be still and know that I am God'. The most profound healing, the greatest light, shines in us when we give up our effort, when we stop thinking. As Edward Carpenter writes:[51]

COINCIDENTAL THOUGHTS

- Those seeking help from you may well be the source of your salvation.
- Life brings together those who need to meet.
- Love not only reaches beyond our ken, but also enables us to glimpse the previously invisible.
- A dark room may be flooded with light if you open the door.
- Tell everyone what you want to do. Many will want to help.
- What are you pretending you can't do?
- What is it you are saying is impossible?
- Are you learning all you can from life?
- How many times are you denying love?
- When life knocked at your door, did you turn it away because it wasn't dressed smartly?

> Of all the hard facts of science, I know of none more solid and fundamental than the fact that if you inhibit thought (and persevere) you come at length to a region of consciousness below or behind thought, and different from ordinary thought in its nature and character. It is a consciousness of a quasi-universal quality, and a realisation of an altogether vaster self than that to which we are accustomed.[52]

The difficulty is that we often make an effort to give up effort. Three helpful methods to move beyond this are:

1. While in a relaxed position, keep your attention firmly on your physical sensations and shape. Drop muscular effort and pass your attention over your body again and again. If you find yourself lost in thought or fantasy, bring your attention back to your body. Be aware of the sensation of your clothing, your separate fingers and toes, what residual expression might be on your face, what you are doing with your tongue. Keep at it for at least twenty minutes.

2. Sit in a comfortable upright position. Then just listen without any attempt to analyse or judge. Hear the inner sounds of your ears if external sounds are low enough. Bring your attention back again and again to sound, to listening. As with the method above, the idea is to take your attention away from thinking and speculating.

3. Sit comfortably and upright. Slow your breathing. Very gently, and without struggle, make your breath as slow as possible. Keep your attention only on the slowness of your breath. Feel the wonderful quietness that enters your being as the breathing slows. Let this quietness pervade you. At first only practise for five minutes, but gradually lengthen the period. Paul Brunton's book *The Secret Path* explains this approach in more detail. [53]

Using any one of these techniques frequently will gradually lead you to a different experience of waking consciousness. You will enter into a sleep-like state but remain awake. Perhaps the boundaries usually given by your awareness of your body will disappear, and you will feel as if you are huge, or floating in space. This is due to your sense of arms, legs and trunk disappearing. There is no need to do anything in this state, simply observe it. But if you are seeking some change or answer to a question, it is very potent to gently hold the question, or image of what you want, while in this condition.

Be still and know that I am God

You will know when you begin to touch the ocean of life with your personal awareness, because the links between yourself and others will become more apparent. Coincidences will emerge in your life. Other signs are that you will discover a feeling of kinship with nature, or the animals, or maybe you will feel it as an awe or even wonder at what you sense is underlying physical nature. This awakening sense will allow you to see behind the scenes that are the only things other people see. This waking sense will feel sometimes like a religious feeling, a certainty that you are connected with everything in a most profound way. It has many stages and aspects, but basically it calls you to accept your connection with all things, and be a willing part of life, not at war or in opposition, or isolated by fear or suspicion that life will swallow you uncaringly. There are levels of advance or initiation into this mystery of waking up to the connection with all things. In the first level we need only to live, work, trade and create in everyday life. If we can do that without harming others, without manipulating them towards their own detriment, without being motivated only for our own needs, then we are allowed into the second gate of the inner city. A friend, Michael Hall, writing about his own experiences after an incident of initiation, says:

> The mystery of life is in all of us. We experience it as the realisation of universality. However, we may shut it out from consciousness by fighting to maintain our separate identity, by struggling just for our own needs, and fending off others through fear or competition. What had happened to me in the tombs was initiation.[54] I saw that the wonderfully common things in life prepare us for this

meeting with the universal within us. Falling in love and caring for another person starts to erode the protection we surround our own identity with. Being a parent and giving oneself to the needs of children takes us further still beyond the isolation of living only for and in oneself. Being a husband or wife who cares for one's partner stretches the fabric of one's psyche to include more than oneself. Through the sympathies aroused one can also begin to empathise with the feelings of other parents, other lovers, other partners. Their loss, their wonder, their tragedy and joy is felt more fully as one's own. And all of this opens one toward the universal spirit of life within oneself. Though imperfect in all my own endeavours in these areas, I had still been helped by them toward finding the wonder of the All within myself.

The common life of love and caring, of social endeavour in service is the path to the wider life of the spirit. Through them you learn the kind of love that transcends one's own small life, and gives you entrance to Life's love.

Life is vital and wondrous. It is just as vital and wondrous, just as physical and subtle as we are. So from a full life one learns to reach up with desire and suck the tits of life. You touch its mystery, roll and fight with it, sit quietly or roar with animal pain. Life is all of these and more. The beautiful sexuality of a man or woman is part of that mystery which we share with each other. It is a part of the universal life. If we are at odds with it, then in some way we are at odds with life. Through loving a person we may fall through our own surface self into the deeps of desire and love that lie behind or around our conscious self. Therefore sex, if it is not for procreation, can be a time of worship.

All these insights into how one touches the universal in oneself suggested the need for touching that Centre, that universal within us. Out of our contact with it arises all our real growth as a person. Without the contact our growth would be stunted or in some way misshapen. With the contact we are more fully expressing what our potential is, and what our fundamental qualities are. I saw how

> my life had led me systematically into greater attunement with the universal in me. I could see how without a sense of one's connection with the central life, we can lack any cohesion with people around us, any real motivation to be a full part of society from other than ambitious or self-centred motives.

Michael's realisation that we all need to touch the Centre from time to time, otherwise we will not grow to our full potential, is vital. But the opposite of it also needs recognition. It is that we are all projections of that one life. So if we shut ourselves off from it, we become less whole, less healthy, less satisfied or productive. Tuning in again allows the obstructions to the light gradually to melt. The greater productivity and satisfaction is not simply to do with earning more money or getting a better job or more social recognition. It has to do with allowing the power of the light to transform the world around you. Its healing, its creativity, can literally change people's lives. It can change the environment around you. This also enables you to know who you are in the wider scheme of things. The result is that you feel more satisfied with life and your place in it.

The healing power

Once you begin to feel the power of coincidence, and see it working, you can begin to allow things into your life, or ask for what you might never have considered before. One of these is the healing of serious or minor ills. Perhaps you had never thought of spiritual healing as a coincidence before. But if you saw someone put their hands on a sick person, and that person was healed with no obvious influence other than the touch of someone's hands, you would be witnessing a healing that coincided with someone's touch.

Such healings synchronise not only with the touch of hands on the sick person's body, but also with a person praying for them, or when the sick person himself earnestly asks for healing. A well-attested example of the latter occurred to a Belgian, Pierre de Rudder.[55] A tree fell on Pierre's left leg, breaking it. The injury was treated by Dr Affenaer. Even after being held in a splint, the leg did not heal, and an open suppurating wound remained on the site of the break. Two centimetres of bone had to be removed, and no connection grew to replace it. Pierre's leg could therefore not support him, and in fact his foot could point only backwards. Other doctors attempted to help, and Pierre told Dr van Hoestenberghe that some weeks after the accident an abscess formed on his lower leg, and out of it came 'a piece of cord'. This was probably one of the extensor tendons, probably the tendon of the great toe, which afterwards remained immobile.

For eight years Pierre and his family survived through the charity of others. Pierre managed to move about slowly with the aid of crutches, dragging his dangling left leg. The wound remained open, and his doctors advised Pierre to allow them to amputate his leg. He refused this, as he said this gave him no hope of ever supporting his family. Instead of amputation he said he would seek healing at a shrine in Oostakker – a grotto similar to Lourdes, but nearer to his home. The journey to Oostakker was difficult. Pierre had to be carried on to the train. People were offended by the smell of his open suppurating wound. The bus from the train to the shrine was also a cause of grievance, and the driver complained about the blood and pus oozing from Pierre's leg and dirtying the bus seats.

At the shrine Pierre begged in his prayers to be allowed to work again. He tried to walk around the cave with the other pilgrims, but had to give up, exhausted. Nevertheless, he felt moved by the atmosphere of the grotto, and through this felt impelled to go to the statue of the Madonna and kneel before it. When he did this, Pierre suddenly realised he had walked to the statue without difficulty. Looking down at himself, he saw that his left leg was supporting him naturally. His wife, who had accompanied him, fainted on the spot when she saw Pierre dancing with joy. In moments the leg had become completely normal. Both legs were now the same length, and the wounds were healed with scar tissue formed.

When he returned home Dr Affenaer wept when he examined Pierre's leg. Dr van Hoestenberghe, a very scholarly man, refused at first to examine Pierre, as he insisted such healing was impossible. In fact he found the bone completely joined, smooth and strong. Pierre immediately started work again as a farm labourer, and lived till he was 75. After his death Dr van Hoestenberghe gained permission to do an autopsy on his body. He found that a healthy piece of bone, two inches long, joined the previously broken bones, and these still showed signs of previous breakage.

Like any wonderful coincidence, Pierre's immediate healing is an anomaly. It completely contradicts what most of us believe is possible in what is often called 'the real world'. When confronted by people who believe in such miracles as the one Pierre experienced, they might even say, 'get real'. This is strange because it is the view that such things cannot happen that is unreal. When we realise that the so-called 'solid' physical world is in fact very plastic and changeable, then we begin to 'get real'. Perhaps the reality is that the core of our being, the light, or spirit, whatever name we give it, projects our body and all the world, like a moving image projected on a screen. The power of the light can change that image in an instant. Beyond time and space it can weave wonders that become apparent instantly in time and space.

There are thousands of examples like Pierre's that could be quoted, from all cultures and times. But Michael Talbot describes an interesting case.[56] Vittorio Michelli was admitted to hospital with a severe cancerous tumour on his left hip. Within ten months the tumour had developed so fast that the joint and hip socket had been completely eaten away, leaving the top of the femur floating in soft tissue.[57] Like Pierre, Vittorio sought healing at a holy shrine – this time at Lourdes. After bathing in the water Vittorio felt unusual heat stream through his body. He bathed several more times and returned home. His healing was not immediate, but over several months the bone and hip completely regenerated, as shown in the accompanying X-rays. The fascinating part of the case is that Talbot continues:

> In a truly stunning example of synchronicity, while I was in the middle of writing these very words, a letter arrived in the mail informing me that a friend who lives in Kauai, Hawaii, and whose hip had disintegrated due to cancer has also experienced an 'inexplicable' and complete regeneration of her bone. The tools she employed to effect her recovery were chemotherapy, extensive meditation, and imagery exercises. The story of her healing has been reported in the Hawaiian newspapers.

Two things need a mention here. One is that many of us may link such miracles with God or orthodox religion. However, it must be remembered that these radical changes occur within and outside of the religious environment. They also occur within any of the religions. The story of Pierre illustrates the healing happening within the beliefs and imagery of the Catholic Church. But the healing that Talbot's friend experienced occurred within the approaches offered by orthodox medicine allied with meditation and the power of imaging change. It is important to recognise that the power of such change in our life is not confined to any particular belief or religion, or even any particular therapeutic approach.

Secondly, we do not yet know precisely what the principles are that produce such amazing healing. The surface differences in the healing of Pierre and the case mentioned by Talbot show that the same thing can happen in apparently different ways. We cannot therefore produce such healing by the application of known principles. We can realise, however, that we each have the potential for radical change, and move towards it in some degree. If we acknowledge that as the principles producing the change are not clear, we may need to try different approaches to find what works for us.

Whatever it is that tunes us in to the power of healing and change, it *can* perform miracles. Whether it is a group of people praying for us, a powerful request or longing on our own part, or the force of directed mental imagery, we can release the transforming power to find healing or life change. The change that comes might be an immediate miracle, or it might be a slow miracle. Fast or slow – it can happen.

People often hold back from asking for such healing, or seeking it for a friend or loved one, because they feel to get it or to be a channel for it, you must be someone special. That is not the case. The existence of your body, and your self awareness, is a miracle. You perform miracles every day. When you decide to reach out a hand, and then your arm extends through space, that is a miracle. When you think of something, then speak it to someone, that is a miracle. When you make love and a baby is later born, that is a miracle. Healing only needs you to reach out a hand, and place it on your sick friend with the knowledge that life itself is miraculous, for healing to take place. There is no need to make any effort or strain at it as if you were producing it. That is a nonsense of egotism. A coincidence arises out of a mysterious conjunction of parts. Being sincere might be a factor – but struggling to make it happen can only get in the way.

Something that happens as your awareness widens to include your connection with the rest of the world, is that you realise you are not alone – have you ever been? You are a co-creator in life, not *the* creator. Whatever happens comes about through a conjunction of many parts. It is the co-operation and unity of these parts that creates an effect. So you are never in control, you are only ever part of an action, even if you initiated it. If you are riding a horse, when you and the horse are in harmony, you can let go of the reins. If you and the horse are in conflict, then perhaps it is relevant that you struggle with the reins, and try to keep control.

Healing, of someone else, or of yourself, also illustrates the games we play that need to be acknowledged. Our deepest wish may not be to help a person towards health, but to be admired, or to feel we have some special quality. Your drive may be to get some sort of self-esteem out of being needed by others. If that is the case, it is much better to admit your need rather than to claim to be, or attempt to be, a healer. You can then be clearer about what you are asking for. Needing acclaim is not wrong. So letting the light into yourself will begin to uncover the fears and power responses you may previously have kept unconscious. While you are asking for one thing, but unconsciously desiring something else, your energy is divided. All of us meet certain critical challenges in our growth, and how we meet these challenges determines how we deal with adult life. For instance, we all attempt to bond with our parent or carer as a small child. We all attempt to become independent, or are faced by independence when the parent or carer dies or is distanced. Our level of success or failure in these areas determines how we relate to people intimately in adulthood. Such learnt responses also determine how well or badly we relate to our own inner energy and potential.

Masters of coincidence

Having led groups for over twenty years, in which people explored their boundaries and went beyond them, I know that in certain states of mind coincidences occur much more often. Part of this is undoubtedly due to the fact that when we are very open and flowing with feelings, we experience the world differently. We notice more. Whatever it is, at such times people say things, a song pours out of the radio, an event occurs, that dovetails completely with what is happening to us. But some remarkable people appear to be in this heightened state much of the time. Padre Pio, the famous Italian priest, so frequently interacted with people in this way, he has been called by many a modern saint. Cecil Humphrey-Smith, who had a bad car accident while working as a quality control inspector for Heinz in Italy, suffered a serious brain condition from the crash. He was ill with uncontrollable seizures for some years. Then, while standing near Padre Pio one day, the priest gently tapped Cecil's head as he passed, and the brain condition was healed from that moment on. [58]

From childhood, Sai Baba of Puttaparte, in India, was surrounded by similar synchronistic events. Still alive today, he has thousands of times waved his hands in the air and solid objects have appeared. A friend of mine, Phil Bradbury, recently wrote me about his own experience of Sai Baba. While travelling with a friend, he stayed for a night at a Sai Baba temple in Srirangapatnam, 30 miles north of Mysore. The next morning the temple keeper offered to show them a holy locket that Sai Baba had blessed. Phil wanted to see this and describes what happened:

> I was expecting to be shown into some ill lit temple and see a dubious object in a glass. The temple keeper, Halagappa, (apparently a reformed thief) was obviously very pleased that we were showing an interest and took us into his shrine room. In there he showed us the *vibhuti* (sacred ash) which collects on the glass

LETTING COINCIDENCE INTO YOUR LIFE

- Keep contact with as many people as you can. The more people you know, the more they can help you 'by chance'.
- Accept responsibility for your life. What you are responsible for you can change or direct.
- Accept the challenges and people life brings you by chance. Take hold of them, recognising their importance.

As suggested by Alan Vaughan

> on the picture of Sai Baba. This didn't mean a whole lot to us but then he picked up this little tin cup and saucer and we went out into the daylight. Inside the cup was a liquid and at the bottom was an oval enamelled medallion about the size of a 1p with Sai Baba's familiar face on it. Halagappa got it out with a teaspoon, drained off the liquid and placed it at the base of my thumb in my upturned hand. There, once the liquid clinging to it had drained into the centre of my palm I could see that it was continuing to drip at the rate of say one drop every three or four seconds! Halagappa said 'drink!' so I tasted this wonderful honey/rosewater liquid – nectar! I held this locket and watched in wonder for at least ten minutes, until Steve insisted on his turn. The centre of my palm was full of liquid!

The medallion is still there. It is still oozing sweet water for no apparent reason, other than that Sai Baba blessed it. Phil adds:

> Devotees who have seen Sai Baba materialise watches, statues, *vibhuti*, sweets, necklaces, or stop the rain, raise the dead, etc., say that they still have moments of doubt, like perhaps they dreamt it or they were hypnotised or it was wishful thinking blah blah. With the locket experience it is 100 per cent, cast iron, kind of matter of fact stuff. It's just that the world – your world – is changed irrevocably. You then go off and try to integrate that experience in some meaningful way into your life or some such response.

Your own personal miracle

Masters of coincidence are not on every street corner. But the world around you speaks to you with the same sort of wondrous strangeness. Why have you met this person at this time? Why did that child smile at you? How come nobody on this street even looks at you? Why did you miss that train? Why did that dog go past just as you left your house?

Perhaps there is no way that we can actually answer those questions fully, or know why each day strangers pass us just in the order they do. But we can learn to look a bit more attentively to what happens to us each day. And we can keep open to those special and personal miracles we call coincidence.

The great masters of coincidence, such as those just mentioned, or people like Edgar Cayce or Eileen Garrett, all tell us that we can move more fully beyond the limitations of the generally accepted world. In the material view of the world, medallions do not produce liquid year after year without some sort of trick. That trick usually needs more than an old tin cup and an empty hand to produce. In the materialistic view, missing bones cannot be regenerated instantly. People do not knock on your door in answer to a prayer.

But in the *real* world, miracles happen. A wonderful connection links us all. Prayers are answered. Healings can take place. Coincidences occur. Why not let them happen to you?

How?

Leave the door of your heart open to the Mystery. Make sure you have opened that door each day.

Notes

1. Reported in *Coincidences* by Ken Anderson. Blandford, UK, 1991. ISBN: 0-7137- 2523 0
2. Reported in the *Evening Standard*, 28.5.99 in a feature by John Hind entitled *On Coincidences*. Also more fully in *Coincidences* by Ken Anderson
3. Sandra and David are fictitious names. Reported in *Coincidences* by Ken Anderson
4. Reported in *Soul Moments* by Phil Cousineau. Conari Press, USA
5. *Closer to the Light*, by Melvin Morse MD, with Paul Perry. Ivy Books, USA. ISBN: 0-8041-0832-3
6. If you wish to explore this information further, read *Synchronicity, Science and Soul-Making* by Victor Mansfield. Open Court, USA. ISBN: 0-8126-9304-3 Call toll-free: 1-800-815-2280
7. References to people, subjects and authors in the boxes. A more complete, detailed description about Bell's Theorem and the 'new' physics can be found on Dr Nick Herbert's web page: http://mail.cruzio.com/~quanta /index.htm :– Michael Talbot is the author of *The Holographic Universe*, published by Grafton Press. See a description of Bell's Theorem on: http://mail.cruzio.com/~quanta /bell.html – See Fritjof Capra's book *The Tao of Physics – Wholeness and the Implicate Order* by David Bohm. Routledge. ISBN: 0415119669
8. Reported in *Incredible Coincidences* by Alan Vaughan. Ballantine Books, USA. ISBN 0-345-35972.0
9. Reported in *Incredible Coincidences* by Alan Vaughan
10. Quoted from *Environmental Science*. Edited by G. Tyler Miller, Jr. Wadsworth Publishing Company, 1999, USA. ISBN: 0-534-53546-1
11. From *Saved by the Light*. Wheeler Pub. ISBN: 1-5689-51191
12. *There Is a River* by Thomas Sugrue. Published by ARE Press. ISBN: 0876041519
13. From *Man and His Symbols* by

Carl Jung. Aldus, UK, 1964
14. Reported in *Soul Moments* by Phil Cousineau
15. This case and other information from Dr Morse can be found on: http://www.death-dying.com/articles/visions.html
16. See Dr Bucke's book *Cosmic Consciousness*
17. 'And God said, Let us make man in our image, after our likeness.' Genesis 1:26
18. Apocryphal New Testament 2:10
19. Matthew, 25:04
20. *Courage* is the name of a beer in the UK
21. The presidential prediction appeared in *Psychic*, August 1976
22. This is more fully explained in my books *Mind and Movement*, and *Liberating the Body*. Or go to http://dreamhawk.com/waves.htm
23. It was also described in *Incredible Coincidences* by Alan Vaughan
24. See http://dreamhawk.com/seed.htm and http://homepages.nildram.co.uk/~jomay/process.htm
25. This is described in my books *Mind and Movement*, and *Liberating the Body*. Also see http://dreamhawk.com/lb-2.htm
26. 'Are not two sparrows sold for a farthing? and one of them shall not fall on the ground without your Father. But the very hairs of your head are all numbered. Fear ye not therefore, ye are of more value than many sparrows.' Matthew 10:43. 'Inasmuch as ye have done it unto one of the least of these my brethren, ye have done it unto me.' Matthew 25:40
27. From *The Mystery of the Mind*, by Wilder Penfield. ISBN: 0 691023603
28. See *There Is a River* by Thomas Sugrue. See http://www.are-cayce.com/
29. Reported in *Coincidences* by Ken Anderson
30. Wakan Tanka can be translated as World Mind, or Wholeness, as used in this book
31. From *Black Elk Speaks* by John Neihardt. Pocket Books, New York, 1959
32. From *The Tao of Physics* by Fritjof Capra. Flamingo, UK, 1976. ISBN: 0-00-654489-4
33. From *The Way to Christ* and *Signature of All Things* by Jacob Boehme. See http://ccel.wheaton.edu/boehme/supersensual_life/supersensual_life.txt
34. From *The Lightening Bird* by Lyall Watson. Hodder and Stoughton, UK, 1982

35. From *Synchronicity: An Acausal Connecting Principle*, by Carl Jung
36. Taken from P. H. Atwater's *Coming Back to Life* but quoted from an article in *Time Out*, November 7-14 1990 entitled *Nearly Departed*, by Colette Maud
37. False name given by author
38. Reported in *Small Miracles II*, by Judith Leventhal, Yitta Halberstam. Published by Adams Media Co. ISBN: 1 580620477
39. The false name of Carol is added by the author
40. Paraphrased from *Closer to the Light*, by Melvin Morse MD, with Paul Perry
41. See *Realms of the Human Unconscious*, by Stanislav Grof; *LSD Psychotherapy* by W. V. Caldwell; *Myself and I*, by Constance Newland
42. See *Realms of the Human Unconscious*, by Stanislav Grof
43. Andrea is a false name given by the author
44. Paraphrased from *Closer to the Light*, by Melvin Morse MD, with Paul Perry
45. Franklin is a false name given by the author
46. See *Is There Life After Death*? by Robert Kastenbaum. Rider; *Death Society and Human Experience*, by Robert Kastenbaum
47. See http://www.netstoreusa.com/tubooks/155/1555171443.shtml for more information about the bombing in Cokeville. *When Angels Intervene to Save the Children; The Cokeville, Wyoming Bombing Incident*, by Wixom, Hartt. CFI Cedar Fort. ISBN: 1555171443. Also reported in *Closer to the Light* by Melvin Morse MD, with Paul Perry
48. *You Can Heal Your Life*, by Louise Hay. Eden Grove, UK. ISBN: 1 870845 01 3
49. From the *Zenkrin kushu*
50. Reported in *The Truth in the Light*, by Peter and Elizabeth Fenwick. Headline Books, UK. ISBN: 07472 4668 8
51. Author of many books on political commentary, anthropology, mysticism and poetry. See Carpenter, Edward. *Civilisation: Its Cause and Cure*. Swan Sonnenschein & Co.; and *Towards Democracy*, Fisher Unwin
52. From Edward Carpenter, *My Days and Dreams* (1916)
53. Paul Brunton's book is ISBN: 0712634215. For details see: http://www.amazon.co.uk/exec/obidos/ASIN/0712634215/qid=937822661/sr=1-30/026-5299354-8424807
54. Michael had been in the

ancient burial tombs in Ireland

55. See http://abbey.apana.org.au/bvm/Bernadette/Derudder.htm where a full report appears. It is also reported in *Amazing Coincidences* by Alan Vaughan
56. Michael Talbot is the author of *The Holographic Universe*, Grafton Press. ISBN 0-24-13690-1
57. X-rays in the book illustrate this unmistakably
58. See any of the following web sites for further information about Padre Pio.
http://www.padrepio.com/
http://www.padrepio.net/
http://www.padrepiocenter.org/

Index